THE SCIENCE
OF MAKING
THINGS HAPPEN

THE SCIENCE OF MAKING THINGS HAPPEN

Turn Any Possibility into Reality

KIM MARCILLE ROMANER

New World Library
Novato, California

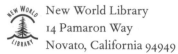 New World Library
14 Pamaron Way
Novato, California 94949

Text design by Tona Pearce Myers
Illustrations by Hiram Henriquez, h2hgraphics.com

Library of Congress Cataloging-in-Publication Data
Romaner, Kim Marcille.
  The science of making things happen : turn any possibility into reality /
Kim Marcille Romaner.
    p.   cm.
Includes bibliographical references and index.
ISBN 978-1-57731-853-8 (pbk. : alk. paper)
 1. Change (Psychology) 2. Success. 3. Self-actualization (Psychology)
I. Title.
BF637.C4R66 2010
158—dc22   2010001710

First printing, May 2010
ISBN 978-1-57731-853-8
Printed in the United States on 30% postconsumer-waste recycled paper

For Zack

CONTENTS

ACKNOWLEDGMENTS

I GRATEFULLY ACKNOWLEDGE THE GUIDANCE, laughter, and support of my editor, Stephanie Gunning, without whom this book would be something else entirely. Also the persistent nature of my agent, Stephany Evans, who was unwilling to let me write it down and then not share it with the world. Finally, thank you to Michael for loving me and reminding me to trust the universe as my partner.

INTRODUCTION

Discovering the Science of Making
Your Dreams Come True

DOES SCIENCE HOLD THE ANSWERS to creating change in our lives? That's the main question I set out to answer when I started writing this book. Scientists are making discoveries on the quantum level of the universe every day. It seems unlikely that what can affect the world on the microscopic level doesn't also have an impact on larger things like human beings. But through what mechanisms?

Coming from the business world, as a technologist, strategist, and innovator, I've always been fascinated with cutting-edge discovery, and I'm constantly studying it. My job often has been to research and explain the latest advances in science and technology to my colleagues and clients, so that we can figure out ways to practically apply them. In my reading I came across the concept of amplification: starting with something small and turning it into something huge. The more I studied its many applications, the more exciting I found the idea. Amplification can turn a whisper into a shout, a dim light into a laser beam, a snowball into an avalanche, and a pale dream into a bold vision. Even more intriguing, physicists use the term *amplify* to describe the process by which quantum possibility becomes reality. Amplification seemed to be the answer to the question "How can we tap the enormous potential available at the quantum level of the universe to make big changes in our lives?"

I dove into the latest research in a variety of sciences and discovered four other building blocks to support what I call the Possibility Amplification Process. As I have shared these ideas with the people I counsel, they've been able to make great use of them in creating success for themselves in all areas of their lives.

Long before I introduced these ideas to my clients, though, I experimented with them myself. I've read hundreds of popular books about creating the life of your dreams, and concepts in these books intrigued me. Because I'm a practical person, however, I wanted to know: is there a science to turning your desired possibilities into reality? So I began my quest to find out. But even before that, three events in my life shaped the nature of this book.

First, I was hit by a truck. Literally. Two weeks after separating from my husband of eight years, I had a head-on collision with an eighteen-wheeler. That these two incidents happened so close together resulted in the biggest transition of my life. Among the broken things were my neck, my sternum, my marriage, my social life, and my ability to work. I was self-employed and a freshly single parent of a three-year-old boy. My decision to keep the house we had lived in as a family seemed idiotic, as I would have to struggle to pay with one salary what used to be covered by two. It was due only to the loving support and generosity of my family that I was able to physically and financially survive this time.

In the months I spent recuperating, I thought a lot about what had to come next if I was to avoid sinking into the mire. I had always imagined I would have a reasonably linear life — one in which I would be married forever, for example — and that it would proceed pretty much as it had up until that point. I really hadn't expected my life to take a hard left turn. I was unprepared.

During my recovery, as I sat at sunset on the patio of the home that I wasn't sure I would be able to keep, it all of a sudden occurred to me that the next phase of my life — or my "next life" as I called it — could be completely of my own design. I was excited by the possibility. What if I didn't follow the rules? What if I went with my hunches, with my dreams, with my gut? What if I designed my next life and then set out to achieve it, letting nothing stop me? And what if, after a number of years, I decided to have yet another kind of life? Was there anything to stop me from building life after life, each of them different from the others, and all of them encapsulated in this one life I'd been given to live on this planet? I imagined how content and satisfied I would feel on my deathbed after living such an intentionally designed life. It seemed like an excellent way to live. Staring into the orange glow cast by the setting sun, I could see them there, all of my potential future lives laid out before me, shining like gems.

This image inspired me for years. What I came to realize was that there is a whole universe of possibility out there for the taking, *if only I could figure out how to access it on a consistent basis and bring it to life.*

The second event that helped shape this book occurred seven years later in a philosophy of religion course I took at Barry University in Miami, Florida. We were studying the historic philosophical arguments for and against the existence of God. Before I discuss this, let me say that I am certainly no expert on the existence of God, and that what I am about to describe was a thought experiment only.

For my class project, I decided to refute a particular argument for God's existence, that of Saint Anselm, a Christian philosopher and theologian of the eleventh century. Saint Anselm's argument is tricky. He wanted to prove that God exists not only in the minds of humans but also in reality.

His argument starts with a definition of God. He said that God is a being "than which none greater exists" — meaning, God is the most powerful being in the universe. If God exists only in our thoughts, Anselm argued, then we can imagine another being, a greater being, one that exists both in our minds and in reality. But, his argument continued, that can't be, because God is the most powerful being in the universe. Therefore, Anselm concluded, God must exist both in our minds and in reality. This is difficult to get your head around, but it's an exceedingly successful philosophical argument.

My counterargument was based on the premise that perhaps it's more powerful to exist as a thought in the mind than in reality. Here's a bit of how I presented it to the class.

"Imagine a Coke can." I brought one to the podium to help my audience achieve this. "In reality, this can is red and silver and made of aluminum. But in my mind . . ." I closed my eyes, "this can is now green. Now it's orange. Now it's made of glass. Now it's a four-foot drum. Now it's as skinny as a reed." I opened my eyes.

"This Coke can, when it exists in my mind, can be anything. All possibilities are available, much as a painting while in the artist's mind can be changed or enhanced. The artist can play with the colors, the perspective, and the shadows. She can add or subtract brushstrokes or objects. But once the artist sets paint to canvas, the painting becomes limited. The paint dries, and the painting becomes static. The only way the painting will change in this world is if the artist puts another layer of paint on the canvas and covers up what she has already created. By bringing the artist's image out of her mind and into this three-dimensional reality, she has actually reduced it, not made it greater. If God is the most powerful being in the universe, then all possibilities are available to God. To bring God into this reality is to limit the limitless. Therefore, God must exist only in the mind."

I remember that my professor stared at me after I finished speaking. Finally he said, "There's something wrong with that." His eyes narrowed. "But I don't know what it is." I took the A and went home.

This exercise enlightened me to the fact that all possibilities are available to us as thoughts *first*. Learning to stretch our capacity to envision more and more possibility for ourselves transforms us into more powerful creators. Our dreams can be bigger. The things we choose to bring into this reality are limited only by our imaginations. Our imaginations are limited only by our willingness to expand them.

The third event that helped shape this book was a simple one. I attended a conference with my mother, who is a medical professional: the annual conference of the National Institute of the Clinical Application of Behavioral Medicine. (This is the sort of thing that geeks like me do for fun.) At the conference, I heard about some of the latest work in a fascinating array of sciences: brain research, behavioral therapies, biology, and various modalities of energy healing. It occurred to me that most of the world had no idea of the concepts and research being shared in those rooms. More important, this was a conference about application. There were definite links between the science and the application of that science that the ordinary citizen would benefit from knowing. I wondered what else was out there that could be shared and utilized. It was at this conference that the basic concept of this book took form and blossomed.

So much has happened since that fateful day with the truck and me. I've recovered my health and have run my first half-marathon. Money is no longer a concern. In fact, the universe has become such an abundant place that I'm sometimes surprised by how much it keeps giving me. I'm remarried to a wonderful man. I'm surrounded by a loving collection of friends. My son has blossomed into a charming young man. I travel to exotic places around the world and have high adventures. I've experienced a meteoric rise in my career, and I'm doing exactly what I wanted to do professionally. I'm living the life of my dreams! The fact that I can explain this with science grounds me and makes me confident that this science can help you too. And you don't have to get hit by truck! A personal crisis is not a prerequisite for taking advantage of the principles in this book. All you need is the desire to live your life to the fullest. All you need is a dream.

HOW TO USE THIS BOOK

Why haven't you already brought your dreams to life? Is it because your dreams are not quite in focus? Then understanding the power of observation can help you. Do you hold back from getting a clear picture of what you want so that you won't end up disappointed in yourself or life? Then learning how the brain amplifies even your smallest thought will inspire you. Do you fear what might be waiting for you at the other end of the bridge to your dreams? Then you'll want to read about epigenetics in chapter 3, and about how your personal beliefs impact your results. Or is it more the thought of failing to get there in the first place that stops you from getting too excited about changing your life? If so, you'll find the answer to how to stay on track in the inverse Zeno effect, described in chapter 5.

The collection of science-based tools in this book will help you design, refine, and align yourself with your dreams in order to more easily bring them to life. You will learn how to strengthen the possibilities you want and suppress the ones you no longer want. You will learn how to leverage the environment to help you with your creative process. You will even learn how to accelerate the realization of your dreams and identify what you might be doing right now to slow yourself down. You will begin to recognize the signs of this science at work as you transition from what used to be your "real" life to the life of your dreams.

The big lesson of this book is that the universe is *designed* to make your possibilities come true. In part 1, "The Five Secrets from Science for Creating the Life of Your Dreams," I explain the science behind that statement. In chapter 1 you'll discover your own power to influence the quantum nature of the universe. In chapter 2, you'll learn what makes you capable of turning possibility into reality. Chapter 3 will reveal your ability to override the seeming inevitability of your genetic code. Chapter 4 will show you how the universe turns quantum possibility into reality — and how you can tag along for the ride. And in chapter 5, you'll learn that physicists have figured out how to speed up a quantum process, and how you can use the same method to speed your progress toward your goals. You will find that throughout the book I have cited the work of many researchers and pioneers who are discovering and applying this science.

In part 2, "Applying the Five Secrets from Science in Your Life," each chapter will guide you intentionally and scientifically to improve your finances, career, love life and relationships, health and fitness, and community involvement. You will also find a collection of tools to help you use this science in productive ways.

What happens at the quantum level of the universe *can* make a difference in your life. Take your dream and combine it with this science, and make it happen!

PART I.

THE FIVE SECRETS FROM
SCIENCE FOR CREATING
THE LIFE OF YOUR DREAMS

1. CHOOSING WITH THE UNIVERSE

Possibility Served Up on a Platinum Platter

FROM THE MOMENT YOU WERE CONCEIVED, you've been swimming in a sea of possibility. You are constantly surrounded by invisible and unlimited possibility, the brilliant and untapped potentiality of the universe. Possibility pulses inside you, waiting for the signal to explode into the world. Possibility, as a quantum physicist would put it, is being *amplified* into reality every second all around you. Are you watching for it? Can you see it?

In that sea of possibility lies your dream. It's right there, waiting for you to choose it, waiting for you to turn on the magnificent power inside you that can bring it to life. Right beside it are the dreams you haven't allowed yourself to have yet, the bigger, bolder versions of your dream that I encourage you to discover and embrace with all your being.

In this chapter, I show you how to drench yourself in possibilities, and how to take the first steps in selecting the ones that have the most meaning for you. You'll learn how to expand your awareness of the possibilities available to you while, at the same time, consciously and deliberately selecting some and discarding others. By choosing, you define your destination and kick off what I call your Possibility Amplification Process. This book will teach you how to get the most from that process. But first you must select from this unlimited sea. You can't amplify something that you haven't first selected.

The truth is that the universe is made up of possibility, and through our conscious and deliberate observation we have the power to make the universe choose specific possibilities out of all those available and amplify them into reality. In this chapter, I share with you two versions of an experiment that proved this to be true: the double slit experiment with light, and the double slit experiment using individual subatomic particles. This power is fundamental to the realization of your dreams, and it's a power you already possess, just like every other human being on the planet. What you've lacked until this moment is the technology to access it. In this chapter, we take step 1 in the Possibility Amplification Process, and that step is composed of observing, choosing, and recording the possibilities you want to amplify into reality.

My first job is to convince you that the universe is indeed made of possibility, and that you can access it. The experiments I describe in this chapter have been explained and written about many times, and you can find additional information about them in the science section of your local library or bookstore. I present them to you here in order to extract the basic principles of the first step of the Possibility Amplification Process.

THE DUAL NATURE OF EVERYTHING

In the late 1700s, a huge debate was going on in the scientific community. Some scientists said light was made up of "corpuscles," or little clumps of "stuff," and other scientists said light was made of waves. In 1801, a physician and physicist named Thomas Young devised an experiment that answered the question for all time. It's called the double slit experiment.

Young surmised that if light were really made of waves, then it would demonstrate the same properties that waves on the surface of water demonstrate. One of those properties is called interference, which is what happens when two waves run into each other. Young's experiment was designed to test for wave interference in light.

You've probably created wave interference yourself. Imagine this: You're standing on the edge of a calm, quiet pond. In each hand you hold a good-sized pebble. Holding your hands out in front of you, you drop the two pebbles in the pond. As soon as the pebbles hit the surface of the water, rings of ripples pulse outward from the places where the pebbles struck. The rings of ripples grow until finally the ripples from one dropped pebble collide with the ripples from the other dropped pebble. As the ripples collide, the smooth arcs of the ripples break up and the surface of the water where they collide becomes choppy. The two waveforms interfere with each other and become distorted, in some places amplifying each other and in other places canceling each other out. This effect is known as wave interference. Young designed his double slit experiment to look for evidence of light crashing into itself like those ripples on the pond.

You can see in Figure 1 how Young set up the experiment. First he created a barrier with one slit in it, so that the light shining through the slit would be coherent — that is, if light was indeed made of waves, it would come through the slit as a single, coherent wave. The light passing through the slit would then shine on a second barrier with two slits placed close together. As light passed through these two slits and landed on the screen behind it, either it would create two vertical lines of light, or it would show evidence of these two streams of light interfering with each other, just like waves of water do.

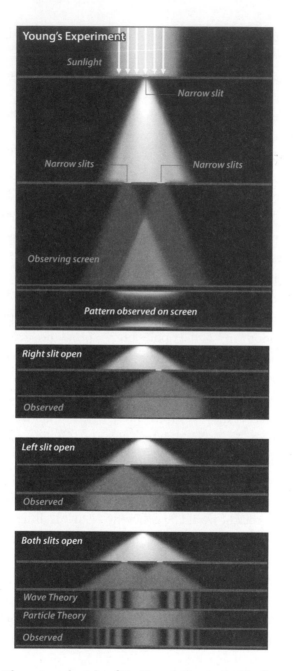

FIGURE 1. *The setup and results of Dr. Young's famous double slit experiment.*

Young discovered that when he made the slits larger and spaced them far apart, two vertical bands of light would appear on the screen. This is what physicists who believed light was made of particles would expect. It's also much like dropping a pebble in a pond while your friend drops a pebble at the same time on the opposite shore of the pond. The waves from your pebble disperse before they can interfere with the waves caused by your friend's pebble, so far away.

But as he made the slits smaller and moved them closer together, *multiple* bands of light appeared on the screen, rather than just two. Young knew that this kind of pattern could only be caused if light was made of waves. As the wave of light passing through one slit collided with the wave of light passing through the other slit, the two waves interfered with each other. Some parts of the light waves were amplified, and some were cancelled out, causing alternating bands of light and dark on the screen. If he closed one of the slits, the multiple bands of light disappeared and just one band of light appeared on the screen. That's what Young expected, since there was only one wave and no interference.

It took many years for the scientific community to accept the fact that light is indeed made of waves, but eventually the conclusion became inescapable. In the years that followed, evidence to support the particle nature of light also mounted. What we know today is that light is made of both waves and particles, but even more important, that *everything* is made of both waves and particles. Every subatomic particle demonstrates the properties of both, whether that subatomic particle is part of a beam of sunshine or part of your shoe.

Now, why would the universe be constructed in such a way that it would need two modes? Let's take the science a little bit further.

THE POWER OF OBSERVATION

In the twentieth century, physicists were able to take Young's experiment to the next level by firing one photon — or particle — of light at a time through the slits. They did this using a photon gun.

Imagine for just a moment that the scientists were using a real gun, rather than a photon gun, to fire bullets at two vertical slits in a wall. Any bullet that made it through one of the slits would embed itself in a barrier on the other side of the wall. The pattern that would eventually build up on the barrier would look like the one in Figure 2.

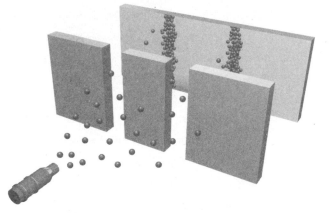

FIGURE 2. *What would happen if real bullets were fired from a gun at the double slits?*

If you were firing one photon at a time from a photon gun, wouldn't the results be the same? It turns out that the answer is no. The physicists watched in amazement as, over time, what built up on that back barrier (in this case, a piece of photographic film) was instead a wave interference pattern. You can see what that looks like in Figure 3.

But wait a minute. What were the individual photons interfering with? If they were being fired one at a time, they each had to choose only one slit to pass through ... didn't they? Or was it possible that one photon could pass through both slits simultaneously?

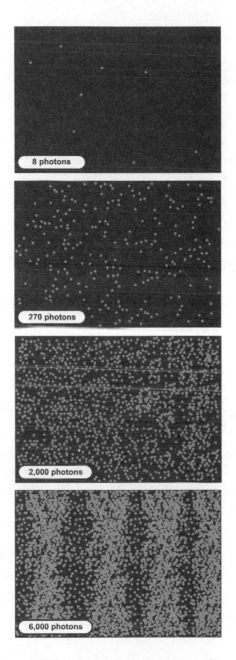

FIGURE 3. *The wave interference pattern appears when subatomic particles are fired one at a time at the double slits.*

The physicists decided to check. They closed one of the slits. When they did so, all the photons passed through the single slit, one after the other, and landed in a bullet-type arrangement on the screen beyond the slit, just like in Figure 2. In other words, the photons acted like particles instead of waves. So what was happening when both slits were open? In order to find out, the physicists used a recording device to determine through which slit each photon actually went.

This is where it gets even crazier. When the physicists watched to see which slit the photons passed through, the photons acted like bullets again and created a pattern like the one in Figure 2. When the recording device was turned off, the photons went right back to behaving like waves and built up a wave interference pattern like the one in Figure 3. *It was as if the photons knew we were watching.*

This experiment has been done over and over, around the world, using not only photons but also electrons, which are particles from the atoms that material objects, like your shoe, are made of. Richard Feynman, a Nobel Prize–winning physicist, said in his physics lecture series at the California Institute of Technology during the early 1960s that in this quantum mechanical experiment is "a phenomenon which is impossible, absolutely impossible, to explain in any classical way, and which has in it the heart of quantum mechanics. In reality, it contains the only mystery." By *classical*, Feynman means according to the physical rules that govern our everyday world. Specifically, the phenomenon to which Feynman refers is: observation modifies outcome.

Wow. Think about what that means: just looking at the universe changes the way it behaves. Let's review for a moment. If both slits are open, even a single photon or electron fired at a time demonstrates its wave properties — by spreading out, keeping loose, and behaving more like a smear of energy than a defined dot. In a way, it's as if the photon is keeping all its options open. But if we record or observe which slit the subatomic particle goes through, it abandons its wavelike properties, becomes a solid particle again, and chooses a specific destination. It's almost as if, by recording what "choice" the particle makes — which slit it goes through — the observer creates a history for the particle that it can't escape and, in this way, affects its future.

The dual nature of the universe and the impact of our observation on that nature are at the heart of accessing possibility. Using the strengths of both waves and particles, we can begin to amplify our desired outcomes into reality.

WAVE MODE VERSUS PARTICLE MODE

Remember back in high school, when they showed you a picture of an atom? There was a little nucleus at the center, and electrons circled the nucleus in succinct orbits like planets? Well, it turns out that's not really what an atom looks like or how electrons behave. Within a certain distance of the nucleus, the electron is actually *everywhere at once*. A quantum physicist would say the electron is in "all possible states at the same time," creating a "cloud of possibility" around the nucleus.[1] This is known as a superposition. (You'll read more about superposition in chapter 2.)

And it's not just the electron that's in all possible states at the same time and keeping all of its options open. It's *every* particle in the atom. In other words, all subatomic matter is simply a vibrating collection of possibilities. And since everything in the universe is made up of subatomic material, everything in the universe is made up of that possibility. Including you. So, you are in fact a being made of possibility, swimming in a sea of possibility. That's the wave mode.

When the electron — or any other subatomic particle — is in the particle mode, all its other possibilities have been suppressed and only one possibility is selected. Quantum physicists call this "collapsing the state." In particle mode, a choice has been made. After that, all activity is about that singular choice.

There are only a few forces that can cause a subatomic particle to choose one possibility out of all the possibilities available to it. As we have just seen, our observation is one of those forces, and we'll talk more about that in just a minute. First, let's talk about how you can access these modes and use them to your advantage.

GETTING INTO WAVE OR PARTICLE MODE

Electrons, like other subatomic particles, are able to be everywhere at the same time when they are in wave mode. In wave mode, all possibilities are available.

You, too, have a wave mode, when all possibilities are available to you. These are the moments before making decisions, or before choosing your next course of action. When you're in wave mode, it's a great time to imagine the results you want to achieve or the dream you will make come true. The wave mode is jampacked with answers, ideas, and inventions just waiting for you to ask for them.

Getting into wave mode is a function of asking the right questions. Questions that start with "if" are wonderful wave mode kickstarters. Here are some great questions to get you into wave mode:

> If this *could* work, how *would* it work?
> If I *did* know the answer, what would it be?
> If I started today, what could I get done by the end of the week?
> If I had the one critical resource I need to make this happen, what would it be?
> If my dream had already come true, what would my life look like now?

These questions and others like them will catapult you into the realm of possibility. But the most important question of all to ask is: "If I could ask this question in another way, what would it be?" When you start out on your quest for possibility with limitations in your questions, you limit the answers you get back from this process. Let's look at an example of using the wave mode to uncover and access invisible possibilities and, at the same time, look at how to liberate you from limitations in the process: A small business owner has decided that she's not generating enough revenue in her business. She feels strongly that she needs to increase her consulting revenues by ten thousand dollars per month. She sets up a brainstorming session with her staff and asks the question "How can we grow consulting revenues by ten thousand dollars per month?" Lots of ideas are contributed. After the session is over, the entrepreneur reviews the suggestions. None seem to be a ten-thousand-dollar answer, but she hopes that by trying multiple suggestions at once she'll get there. Her confidence that she'll achieve her goal is something less than 100 percent.

Can you see how she limited the answers she got back? She started out by asking how to grow consulting revenues. If she'd asked instead "How can we grow *revenue* by ten thousand dollars per month?" and not limited the question to consulting, new revenue streams might have been invented right in that meeting. Perhaps the additional revenue burden could have been shared by different products or services offered by the company. And if the ultimate goal behind increasing company revenues by ten thousand dollars a month was to put five thousand dollars more per month in her own pocket, imagine what possibilities might have opened up by specifically asking how to do that. For example, she could open a second business, or cut costs, or go work for someone else, or pick up some paid speaking engagements. By deciding in advance how the universe would deliver what she desired, she cut off other possibilities that would work perfectly well.

You can see how quickly our small business owner moved from strategically looking at the possibilities for increasing income to the tactical solutions. She had the right idea in setting up a brainstorming session, but she was brainstorming at too low a level. She'd already decided some of the variables. The wave mode is about expansiveness, about opening up all the doors and windows and seeing what flies in.

I once questioned Margaret Atwood, the famous author of *The Handmaid's Tale* and many other works, about where she gets her ideas. She said, "Put your left hand on the table in front of you, put your right hand in the air . . . and stay that way. You are now a conductor of ideas. Ideas will begin swooping through you. If an idea happens to swoop through your mind, you can capture it and use it. It's yours."

To be a conductor of both possibility and ideas, ask the most unlimited questions you can imagine, and give yourself plenty of time to receive the answers. You might even ask some of the same questions twice, in different sessions at different times, to see what new possibilities have arisen in the meantime.

The particle mode is about tactics, and it's easy to get into: Make a decision. Choose. With that one act, you collapse all the possibilities into one. This is the signal to both yourself and the universe that you are now ready to turn your chosen possibility into reality. Everything after that is tactical action. Do your part by participating fully in your choice and you'll be amazed at how the universe responds.

If you're hovering at this moment between choices, you may be wondering how you can be sure you're making the right decision. Here are three ways to tell:

- Gut check. Use your intuition. Does it feel right?
- Back that feeling up with the facts. Given what you know at this moment, is the decision a reasonable one?
- Ask someone — or several people — you trust.

But is wondering about the rightness of your decision the right wondering? The truth is, you could spend your whole life wondering at the rightness or wrongness of a particular decision. If you've been wondering for years if you should leave your significant other, then it's probably time to go. No amount of additional wondering is going to make you happier in your relationship. At some point, it becomes extraordinarily advantageous to your mental health to choose and collapse the state rather than keep multiple options open at once. Give yourself a certain amount of time to waffle, and then make the best choice you can. By choosing, you begin to weave your amplification magic.

POSSIBILITY TIP

The wave mode and the particle mode both have positive and negative aspects. To limit the negative aspects, it's best to balance the amount of time you spend in each mode. If you're feeling guilty because you never get anything done, you're probably spending too much time in wave mode. If you're feeling like a hamster on a wheel, you're spending too much time in particle mode.

Now you know that choice is a powerful catalyst in amplifying possibility into reality. Let's turn once again to observation, another tool in our amplification arsenal, and take a look at how it works in our daily lives.

OBSERVATION ALONE IMPROVES RESULTS

Our observation has a powerful impact at the microscopic level of the universe, but it's also an extremely powerful tool at the macroscopic level of the universe, our everyday world. Observation can improve results. A study conducted in Kenya showed that when community healthcare workers were under observation in the hospital, they made fewer treatment prescription errors than when they were out in the field and unobserved. In a study of librarians in the field of health sciences, it's been shown that when librarians are being observed their bibliographic searches return better results than when they're not being observed. Intensive care units in hospitals end up less contaminated when an observer inspects the room after it's been cleaned.

Well, that's great, you may be thinking. But in each of those examples, one person is watching another. Besides the creepy Big Brother implications, is it really necessary to find an official observer to watch over me in order to create the reality I want? Luckily, the answer is no, because you already have two entities constantly observing you.

The first observer is you. Each of us has an internal observer of our own. This internal watcher sees everything you do and notices everything about you. The second observer is the environment. The environment is defined as everything and everybody around you. In chapter 4, I discuss the environment's observational power and how you can leverage it. Right now, I want to emphasize your own power to observe yourself in real time and in the future.

Also known as self-awareness, the concept of the internal observer has existed for thousands of years and is credited to Eastern traditions such as Buddhism and Hinduism. To lead students to a personal understanding of their own internal observer, masters and teachers in these traditions ask questions such as, "When you say, 'I am tired,' who is the 'I' that is noticing you are tired?" The point is that there is a you *being* you, and there is a you *watching* you.

Some people are closely connected to their internal observers and use them to their advantage. Others may have never thought about this division inside themselves, or what it might mean. Whichever group you find yourself in, it doesn't really matter, because whether you have studied the concept or not, the observer within you still exists.

There are several ways we self-observe. We can notice our behaviors and emotions. We can monitor sensations in our bodies. We can critique a past performance or preview our future performance.

For example, I'm sitting here eating a ham sandwich as I write. I made it myself, and it's a rather large ham sandwich. Because I'm writing this passage of self-observation, I have noticed a few things:

- I'm full.
- I feel a desire to keep eating the sandwich because it's tasty and delicious.
- I'm realizing that continuing to eat the sandwich does not line up with my vision of myself as a slim, healthy person.
- I am imagining myself taking some alternative action, such as throwing away the rest of the sandwich or storing it in the refrigerator.

When you take a step back into observer mode, all of a sudden you become aware of your choices and how they affect you. I could easily have decided to remain unaware and eat the rest of the sandwich, only to feel bloated and unhappy about it afterward. Instead, I wrapped up my half-eaten sandwich and stored it for later. By bringing my own focused attention to what I am doing in the moment, I can align my behaviors, thoughts, and emotions with my desired outcomes.

In the earlier-mentioned studies of the observer and the observed, this alignment created optimum results. Having a dream and not being aligned with it will diffuse your energy and slow down your creation process. To counter this effect, you will find a robust collection of tools in chapter 3 to help you achieve personal alignment with your goals.

I strongly recommend that besides observing yourself in real time, you observe yourself in your imagination. Visualization is a cornerstone of the Possibility Amplification Process.

OBSERVING THE IMAGINED SELF

Athletes have long used self-observation in the form of mental imagery or visualization to improve performance. They imagine themselves effortlessly and perfectly executing their sport, handling distractions, and dealing with the unexpected. In a 1987 study of 235 Canadian Olympic athletes who participated in the 1984 Olympic Games in Sarajevo and Los Angeles, mental readiness surfaced as the primary link to medaling, not physical readiness or technical readiness. The subjects of the study were not experts at visualization when they first began using the technique, but they credited much of their success to their ability to master visualization skills. (In chapter 3, you'll find several exercises for improving your own.)

For Olympic athletes, visualization is a key component to making their dreams of winning the games come true. They can attest that vividly imagining their desired outcomes helps make them real.

Visualization is a key component in making your dreams come true as well. You should be able to vividly imagine what it will be like when your dreams have become reality. If you're not clear about what you want, I can guarantee that the universe won't be, either. In the next section, I lay out a process to help you become very clear about the dream life you want to create.

CHOOSING A PORT ON THE SEA OF POSSIBILITY

Designing a vision of the life you wish to create is like looking out the window with binoculars. At first everything is fuzzy, until you adjust the focal point of the lenses to bring things sharply into focus. As your gaze crosses the landscape, you may find that you need to adjust the focal point again because some objects in your field of vision are closer or farther away than your initial point of focus. Some of the objects out there will be uninteresting to you, and you won't choose to focus on them at all. The more often you look out that window with your binoculars, the more quickly you'll be able to focus to optimize your view.

As you imagine the life of your dreams, some parts will be better focused than others. You may see the love of your life very clearly, but your financial future may be blurry. Your health picture may be crisp, but your family life may be a question mark. As you spend time envisioning and contemplating the dreams you have for the various major areas of your life, you will bring those desired outcomes more and more firmly into focus. The more often you envision your desired outcomes, the easier it will be to bring them into focus. And lastly, clearly knowing *which* outcomes deserve your time and attention will make it easier to ignore the distraction of other options.

You know what it's like when you're thinking about buying a new car? When you look around, it seems that your dream car is everywhere. New channels of information about your car suddenly appear. You see the commercials, you visit the websites, and you ask people you don't even know how they like owning it. You learn secrets about your car, its ins and outs. You learn which dealers have provided the best buying experience. You tune in to the different ways you might be able to finance it, coming up with options that might never have occurred to you before. You learn to tune out and not waste time on information about other cars that pale by comparison. And all this is made possible because you clearly focus on your desired outcome. When you get serious about amplifying possibility into reality, the tools you need become available to you.

As author William Gibson, who coined the term *cyberspace* in his book *Neuromancer*, once said, "The future is here already. It's just not evenly distributed."[2] Parts of your vision will materialize from the ether sooner rather than later, seeming more solid to you and more accessible. Others will seem far away and fuzzy. That's okay. Spend some more time on those fuzzier parts and they will become clearer to you, I promise.

The following is a step-by-step guide to designing a destination, the vision of your dream life. The rest of the book will be your navigational chart for getting there.

DESIGNING THE DESTINATION

The available literature about successful mental imagery suggests that the vision you create has to have five characteristics:

IT HAS TO BE POWERFUL. Does it really resonate with you? Does it pull your heartstrings or get you truly excited when you picture it? Does it elicit a passionate response? Zero in on the possibilities that mean the most to you.

IT HAS TO BE EMOTIONAL. We spend a lot of time trying to make ourselves feel better. One goal in creating the life of your dreams is to experience the great emotions that come along with it. Feel the feelings attached to your dreams and they will make your vision even more powerful.

IT HAS TO ENGAGE MULTIPLE SENSES. The more you can experience your vision across all of your senses, the more real it will seem to you.

The better you get at doing this, the easier it will be for you to "cross over" into the life of your dreams.

IT HAS TO DESCRIBE AN END STATE, NOT A PROCESS TO GET THERE. If you are describing a piece of clothing to a tailor whose job it is to make it from scratch, you do not tell the tailor how the sleeves should be attached to the shoulders. You are placing an order. Order what you ultimately want, and leave the sewing to the expert. The universe can deliver possibility via an infinite number of channels, many of which you can't even imagine.

IT HAS TO BE VIVID. Picture your dream life as brightly and with as much detail as you can. Notice the colors and textures. If there's any part of your dream life that's still a bit fuzzy, noticing the details will help crisp it up.

Your vision has to be so strong that the "real" world around you begins to fade away. What is the real world, after all? Your real world is made up of your current beliefs, your current perceptions, and your current understanding of how things are. Basically, the real world is a construct — a vision — that you've developed over time. By creating a new vision, you give your brain the material it needs to begin operating in a different way. In the presence of your future vision, your vision of the present fades away.

How do you create this crystal clear, powerful vision of your dream life?

First, go crazy imagining it. Get into wave mode and dream about the life you will be leading when your dreams have all come true. Choose specific outcomes in the following seven categories, and use the methods that follow this section for recording your vision.

RELATIONSHIPS. In this category, picture all the things you would like to have happen in your various relationships. Are you looking for the love of your life? What are the most important qualities for that person to possess? In order to engage your senses, think about what this person looks like, feels like, smells like, and sounds like. Imagine the emotions you will feel when he or she is near you. Are you crazy in love, excited, comforted, happy? Imagine that you are already with this person, and that your relationship is already just the way you want it. Your dream life is about having that fabulous relationship, not meeting that person. Visualize the end state, not the journey.

Other relationships to consider in this area include those with friends, family, coworkers, your boss, church fellows, and so forth.

FINANCES. What would it be like if you had all the money you would ever need saved up for retirement? What if you could retire right now? How about just paying off those medical bills? Can you feel the relief? The excitement of having more disposable income than you've ever had before? What would you do with it? Would you travel around the world? What kinds of toys would you like to own? A boat? A plane? What experiences would you create for yourself? What experiences would you off-load if you could pay someone else to do them for you?

SPIRITUALITY. You may have dreams of being fully grounded, fully connected to your inner self. You may want to feel closer to the deity of your religion. You might want to experience a greater connection with everything because you believe we truly are all one. (And if you look at it from a quantum perspective, you'd be right: we are all just energy, space, and information.) Perhaps you want to feel more gratitude for the things you already have in life. Imagine how you will feel when you are this connected person. More important, feel those feelings as if you already *are* that person. How do you now carry yourself in the world? How have your activities changed? How do others now view you?

EMOTIONS. Do your emotions sometimes hold you back? I know mine do. What emotions would you like to experience on a daily basis?

What emotions would be better left behind? Are there some emotions that you'd really like to feel but haven't felt at all lately? How would you like to feel when you wake up in the morning? Would you like to experience your emotions without letting them take over? Describe the emotional you that you dream of becoming.

YOUR PHYSICAL BEING. In this area, describe the perfectly healthy, fit you. Perhaps exercise is part of your daily routine. Maybe you'd just like to walk more than you do now. Is it your dream to run a marathon? Improve your golf swing? Increase your flexibility? Be twenty pounds lighter? (Notice that I didn't say, "*Lose* twenty pounds." Remember, you're building a vision of what you've already accomplished.) What kind of diet do you have? How does it make you feel to have the physical capabilities and image of your dreams?

PROFESSIONAL DEVELOPMENT. You've achieved the ultimate in your chosen career. Everything is operating like clockwork. Perhaps you've reached the top of your organization or created success as an entrepreneur. What awards have you won? Are magazine writers calling for interviews? What exactly are you doing? Is it what you're doing now? Is it for the company you're working for now? What kind of freedom is now available to you because of having achieved this professional stature? Do you feel proud? Gratified? Fulfilled? How does your family feel about you? How does that make you feel?

PERSONAL DEVELOPMENT. Would you like to learn a language? Dance salsa? Sail? Play a new sport? Is there a subject you'd like to become the expert on? Perhaps you've always wanted to try making stained glass windows or woodworking. Maybe you'd like to write a book or sing in a jazz club. Whatever new skill set you'd like to develop or underused talent you'd like to explore, capture it here, as if it had already happened. Imagine yourself successfully applying your new skill and how it will make you feel.

DRAWING UP THE ARCHITECTURAL PLANS

When designing the destination of your dreams, you'll want to record all the details. There are so many fun tools available! (Later, I hope to convince you that creating the future of your dreams is both easy and fun.) Here are some of my favorite ways to record the dreams that I intend to bring to life:

GOAL LISTS. If you like bullet points, or if you like to check off your to-dos, goal lists are for you. I have kept goal lists for years. Figure 4 is an example from 2000, which I updated twice.

You can see from the text at the top that I was working on my own belief system in 2000. Since I last updated this list, I've reached several more of these goals. I often went back to review this list, update my progress, and give myself credit for making progress toward my vision. Where I have partially completed a goal, for example, you'll see just a forward slash, not a complete check mark. I also specified in how many years I would complete each goal. You can see that some of my goals were pretty immediate, such as sending Sandi's birthday present. That's because I like the feeling of checking things off. But it's also true that I wasn't thinking big enough when I wrote this list. My vision sheets are much more detailed and ambitious these days.

JOURNALING. Diaries and journals are great places to write the story of your magnificent life. Several years ago, I was inspired to change my journals from tired recountings of the day's happenings to celebrations of everything I consider important. My more recent journals are rich collections of drawings, ideas, quotes, poetry, and stories that deepen my vision. If you want some guidance on getting the most from your journaling, you should check out my friend Sandy Grason's book, *Journalution*.

MULTIMEDIA. Use your artistic capabilities to capture your dream future. I know people who have become millionaires by drawing

2000 GOALS (2000 AND BEYOND!)
(UPDATED 11/12/00) (UPDATED AGAIN 3/1/01)

FAITH
Believe, and it shall be so.
Life is about perception.
I believe I have a great life, and I do.
I believe I can accomplish everything I desire.
I desire the things/states/ideas on this list.

GOAL	YEARS TO COMPLETE
FINANCIAL	
Pay $5,000 down on car in 2002	2 ✔
Save $8,000 in liquid savings	2
Save $200,000 for Zack's college fund	8
Invest $100,000 for retirement fund	4
Enter credit card transactions in Quicken	1 ✔
SOCIAL	
Meet my husband-to-be	1 ✔
Invite people over for two parties (one down!)	1 /
Send Sandi's birthday present	1 ✔
Plan Tammy's birthday celebration	1 ✔
Invite Jordan over to play with Zack	1
PHYSICAL	
Lose five pounds	1
Develop more strength	1 ✔
Work out 3 times a week	1
MENTAL	
Finish portfolio, get bachelor's degree	1 ✔
Get U.S. sailing certification	1 ✔
Get MBA	1
SPIRITUAL	
Visit Karla after surgery	1 ✔
Visit Nancy after surgery... sigh.	1 ✔

FIGURE 4. *A page from my own goal book.*

their dream worlds and then making them come true. The vision board is a popular option these days. Vision boards are created by cutting out magazine pictures that represent your desired outcomes and pasting them on poster board. I actually have mine in a scrapbook. Prefer action? Get out your video camera and describe what your dream life looks and feels like. Take your viewers on a video tour of your creation. Build a website or start a blog and tell people what you intend to create. By engaging others in a conversation about the creation of dreams, you will amplify the energy around your own.

TALK ABOUT IT. You've probably seen both sides of this argument. Some would advise you to keep your dreams to yourself in order to avoid the effects of negative outside forces. My opinion is that belief flourishes when challenged. Every answer you create in response to people who rain on your parade informs and convinces not only them but you too. Tell anyone who will listen about what you intend to create. The wheels of the universe will begin turning on your behalf.

Use more than one of these modalities if you can. Each has its own power. Besides, it's a lot of fun to play around with your imagination. Spend time with your vision and nurture it. It's one of the few things in life that really and truly belong to you and you alone.

Now that you've created and recorded a crystal clear vision of the possibilities you wish to amplify into reality, let's explore your secret power for doing so.

2. YOUR BRAIN ON CHAOS THEORY

A Real, Live Dream Machine

I FLEW THE OTHER DAY.

I wasn't on a plane, nor had I jumped out of a plane. (I would classify that as "falling.") I didn't have any wings. Nonetheless I experienced unaided flight — just the wind and my body.

If you're anywhere near as skeptical as I am, by now you're running through all the possibilities in your brain. "What could she possibly mean? Does she mean . . . she jumped off a cliff? (Falling.) Does she mean . . . she bungee jumped? (Falling.) Does she mean . . . she was dreaming? (It happened in this universe.) Does she mean . . . Well, what the heck *does* she mean?"

Observe: This is how possibility breaks into our minds. Once I tell you how I flew, your understanding of your available options will be expanded. Mine certainly were.

How I flew is called indoor skydiving. It's an activity that takes place in a vertical wind tunnel. When I came out of the tunnel the first time, I was on such a high that I jumped up and down, saying, "I want — to go — again! I want — to go — again!" So, I did. Many times. You can, too. By far, it is one of the coolest things I've ever done.

With every possibility that you add to your list of known pos sibilities, your universe gets a little bit bigger. So here's another possibility to add to your list: creating the bigger, bolder life of your dreams is easy and fun. The universe does not need to make this complicated. It knows what *it's* doing. It only needs for *you* to know what it's doing. Then things will move along much faster.

So let me tell you the secret: You are the best-designed possibility amplifier in the universe. Just as musical amplifiers boost the volume of sounds, in your role as a possibility amplifier you have the ability to turn unrealized possibilities into realities. You can make dreams stronger. In addition, you are capable of seeking out the richest, juiciest, most vibrant possibilities available. Your stray imaginings, wishes, and goals can become ecstatic, sumptuous, powerful visions of the future. With this book as your guide to the amplification process, these visions are the possibilities that you will make real. First, let me tell you about the science of possibility amplification, and then we'll discuss the ways in which you can turn on and intensify your amplification abilities.

Dr. Jeffrey Satinover is my hero. Step-by-step, in his dense yet fascinating book called *The Quantum Brain*, he builds an extraordinary and compelling theory of the brain that says we are the queens and kings of our universe. Basically, our brains are specifically designed to access all the raw quantum possibilities — a subject you just read about in chapter 1 — and to amplify them, producing the results that we experience in our everyday lives. Let me walk you through Satinover's theory and, while we're at it, examine the role that some of these major ideas play in your daily experience.

The first major point of Satinover's theory is that the brain is a chaotic system, and in this belief he is not alone. More and more research points to the fact that the brain, and the nervous system in its entirety, demonstrates the characteristics of chaotic systems.

A chaotic system is one that produces unpredictable results. The same chaotic system can produce very different results, depending on the conditions the system starts with. For example, the repetitive tossing of a coin is a chaotic system. Whether the coin comes up heads or tails depends on how hard it's flipped, how high in the air the coin is tossed, how great the distance to the surface it lands on, whether the coin is damaged in any way, and so forth. We can say that the coin will come up heads or tails approximately half the time, but we can't call any particular flip of the coin with 100 percent certainty.

Despite our inability to predict the exact results a chaotic system will produce, there is an underlying order to all chaotic systems. In amplifying possibility, we take advantage of the order underlying the chaos in our own brains to create the outcomes we want.

Chaotic systems are common. Examples of chaotic systems include our planet's atmosphere, turbulent waterways, the movement of the earth's crust, and human population growth. As we saw in the coin example, one defining feature of chaotic systems is their sensitivity to changes in initial conditions. The butterfly effect is the most commonly known example of this, explaining how a small random event like a butterfly flapping its wings in Africa could cause a tornado in Texas. But let me give you another example you'll perhaps relate to more readily: my house in the morning. Almost everyone who's been to my home at that time would agree it is a chaotic system.

My teenage son, Zack, is hard to wake up. Some days I am more successful at getting him out of bed than other days. On the mornings when he's had enough sleep and wakes readily, it's guaranteed that he will brush his teeth before he leaves the house. On those days he leaves his comforter on the living room couch because he's had time to watch TV while eating his cereal and likes to keep himself warm while doing it. We are both in better moods, because I won't have yelled at him for forty-five minutes straight. He arrives at his homeroom at school on time. On the mornings when he's really hard to get out of bed, however, a fifteen-minute delay could mean no brushed teeth, breakfast in the car, grouchy good-byes, and possibly a Saturday detention, if he's been late to school enough times in a row.

In this chaotic system, Zack could eventually end up with a cavity from not brushing his teeth each morning, a long-term result of a minor change in the time he gets up. But of course, Zack never gets any cavities, making it difficult for me to impress on him the importance of brushing his teeth. After his last uneventful dental checkup, he told me he has "hero teeth." Talk about amplifying possibility!

So the initial condition — whatever time Zack gets out of bed — causes the system of "getting out of the house in the morning" to develop differently from day to day. The results are not necessarily predictable, since there are so many variables. For example, I may have bought breakfast bars at the grocery store this week, so Zack can grab one and eat his breakfast in the car, thereby saving us some time. Or he might have showered the night before, eliminating the need to do so in the morning, and so we recover some of the lost time he spent oversleeping. We don't always need as much time to get ready.

On the other hand, some variables could cost us minutes. There might be a huge traffic jam on the way to school, for instance, which would wipe out the time gain Zack created by showering the night before. On some other mornings, I might be running late or the exterminator might show up unexpectedly, or some other event could take place, causing Zack to be late even if he did get up on time.

In other words, the initial condition of "Zack gets up fifteen minutes late" can eventually create the outcome of "Saturday detention for Zack," but is not guaranteed to do so. Furthermore, although the initial condition of "Zack gets up on time" is more likely to prevent the outcome of "Saturday detention for Zack," it is not guaranteed to do so because of the many other variables involved in the system. You can see, however, that the initial condition of "Zack gets up on time" is far more likely to result in the types of positive outcomes that I, for one, desire. (I dream about the positive outcomes that might result if the initial conditions in this system included "Zack gets up *early*," but so far it's been my dream, not his, and has been negated by *his* dream, "Zack doesn't have to go to school today.")

Second, Satinover says, the brain is an iterative system. Iterative systems are characterized by being repetitive and having feedback loops. In other words, information being processed in the brain is passed back and forth between neurons over and over again, with quite a bit of error-checking on both sides. Chaotic systems that are also iterative are even *more* sensitive to initial conditions than noniterative chaotic systems — and their amplification power is greater as well. So how can you tap into this great power?

Thinking — simple thinking — is the first component in the process by which our chaotic, iterative brains amplify raw, quantum possibility into reality. It is in the creation of a thought — the mere formulation of an idea — that the process of possibility amplification begins.

The second component of the amplification process is choosing: Which thoughts (visions, dreams) will you bring to fruition as tangible results? According to the latest in brain theory, your choices kick-start everything.

CHOICE:
YOUR CHAOTIC BRAIN'S INITIAL CONDITION

Thousands of times a day, we make choices. From among the limitless possibilities available to us, we choose what we think, the words we say, the actions we perform, what we pay attention to and what we ignore, and what to eat for lunch. These choices are among the catalysts that cause our brains to fire off signals to the various parts of our body. These choices are what make things happen in our bodies and in our world.

Friedrich Beck of the Institute of Nuclear Physics at the Darmstadt University of Technology in Darmstadt, Germany, and John Eccles of the Max Planck Institute for Brain Research in Frankfurt, Germany, have developed a quantum theory of brain activity that is completely dependent on our *intentions*. That is, without our first selecting a preference, the brain would not be capable of controlling voluntary action.

Jeffrey Schwartz, Henry Stapp, and Mario Beauregard of the University of California Neuropsychiatric Institute in Los Angeles, the Lawrence Berkeley National Laboratory at the University of California, and the Research Center in Experimental Neuropsychology and Cognition in Montreal, Canada, respectively, have developed a separate quantum model of mind-brain interaction that indicates that without our originating thoughts or intentions, we would be veritable couch potatoes. While the hardwiring of the brain would continue to run the involuntary processes of the body, such as breathing and the beating of the heart, we would do nothing else.

The brain is entirely capable of processing and preparing for every available possibility, but without us choosing which one we want, none can be brought to fruition. It is the mental event — the choice — that serves as the initial condition for a system to emerge (such as what time Zack decides to get up in the morning, or how often you choose to brush your teeth).

You've seen this effect in your own life. Let's say a morning meeting at the office runs long. You've scheduled back-to-back meetings all day, so you watch in dismay as the clock ticks closer and closer to the start of your next meeting. Your brain has been fed one initial condition: a late end to a meeting. What else could you throw in there as fodder for your brain to amplify? Here are four possible emotional choices.

- TRANQUILLITY. You excuse yourself from your meeting and call the person with whom you are meeting next. You tell this person that you will be late, and together you decide on the best way to handle the delay. You return to your meeting.

- PANIC. You believe or feel you can't leave the meeting to make a phone call, so you squirm in your chair and decide to sweat it out until the meeting is over. Then you plan to drive like a madwoman to your next meeting.

- DESPAIR. You allow thoughts to swirl through your mind like a raging tornado. "Nothing ever goes right for me! Why is it always like this?"

- ACCEPTANCE. You decide that fifteen minutes won't make or break the next meeting. You'll be able to finish it on time even if it starts late, and you anticipate that the rest of your day will go swimmingly.

Your day will develop according to which of these responses you choose and feed into the chaotic system that is your brain. The day that starts with the tranquil or accepting response will most probably be less turbulent throughout, and if other unexpected events pop up, you'll be more likely to handle them in the same calm manner. If you choose a distressed, panicky, or worried approach to this starter event, you may find yourself off balance the entire day. In either case, you've started a system that isn't completely predictable, but that has a certain character to the way it will play out.

The critical fact to take from this example is that *the choice to stay calm or not is completely yours*. That's a wonderful position to be in. By choosing, you are in charge of building your daily experience. Through choice, we can improve our chances of having a wonderful day by feeding better intentions into it.

In essence, all of your life is a chaotic system. If you say the wrong thing to your spouse, you might spend the next two hours arguing. If you say just the right thing to your spouse, you could possibly spend the next two hours making love. Or maybe you say the wrong thing, apologize sincerely, and spend the next two hours snuggling on the couch watching a movie together. No matter what choice you make, what happens next — and how you experience it — is a continued series of choices between possibilities. As we saw in chapter 1, choice is the scepter that you, as queen or king of your universe, hold in your hand. Choice not only signifies your power, it is your power.

The beauty of carrying this scepter in a chaotic, quantum universe is that every possibility is available to you, wholly and at once. In fact, the potentiality of the universe floats all around you and within you, invisible. With just a wave of your hand — or your brain — the possibilities that appeal to you can materialize from the ether.

The image of every possibility teeming all around you waiting for your summons may seem a little overwhelming. But remember, there is order in chaotic systems. As you begin the amplification process, your thoughts, your actions, and the environment around you may seem random and unpredictable. Hold fast to your vision of what is to be, use your amplification power to choose the possibilities you want, and you will begin to see the patterns in the seeming randomness.

The third component in the Possibility Amplification Process is action. As Satinover points out in *The Quantum Brain*, we've already inarguably demonstrated our ability to amplify quantum effects to tangible effect in our reality through our actions. When humans shoot subatomic particles through slits and record their landings on photographic material, it's pretty clear that the photographic material and the visible patterns on it are part of our real physical world. Graduate students can arrange subatomic particles into a pattern that spells out the abbreviation of their university's name and take pictures of it with the help of an electron microscope.

But so what? So far nobody has proven that we can control subatomic matter in our everyday lives, have they? Satinover is a member of a group of thinkers who say the brain not only can amplify quantum effects but also is doing it every day. When you think about it, you're moving this big collection of subatomic particles known as your body around every time you walk, sit down, eat dinner, and so on. Every time you fold a piece of paper, the subatomic particles of your hands influence the subatomic particles of the paper. You first think about making the fold, and then the fold appears through your manipulation of subatomic energy.

Wouldn't it be cool if what you really are is a being composed of energy capable of molding other energy into anything you can imagine?

In our thoughts, we humans create emails, meals, furniture, clothing, art, and vacations — and all of these things become tangible experiences in our everyday lives through our actions. In the pages to come, we'll explore how to master the power of possibility amplification to produce the tangible results you want and to downplay or eliminate the ones you don't want.

TWELVE STEPS FOR REACHING ELEVEN ON A DIAL THAT GOES TO TEN

"Hi, my name is Kim, and I'm a possibility amplifier." To master your power to amplify possibility and leave behind your old ways of experiencing the world, you'll have to enroll in my twelve-step program. The purpose of this program is to provide you with a set of tools to maximize the amplifying power of your brain. You won't have to come to meetings, and you won't have to introduce yourself in the traditional twelve-step way, but you will definitely want to read the literature and follow the program. The cool thing is that you can do the twelve steps in any order you choose, and you can revisit them any time you need an amplification boost.

I put Risk Taking 101 at the top because it is a core technique that will serve you in anything you choose to do. Innovating your life absolutely requires it. I focus here on physical risks because taking physical risks requires conscious, focused attention.

Practicing conscious, focused attention can promote change in all areas of your life, and what better way to do it than when you are physically challenged? I guess I could tell you to sit around and meditate, but isn't, say, jumping out of a plane a lot more fun? A recent article in *Psychology Today* tells the story of Annette Van Horn, a woman who learned to trust herself and take charge of her life by learning how to fly a plane. There's no question that in flying a plane you take your life in your hands. As a result, Ms. Van Horn realized that she needed to take control of her troubled marriage, and with her newfound sense of confidence and self, she did so. Get yourself comfortable being on the edge, and change will explode in all areas of your life.

Step 1. Risk Taking 101

Here's something you should know about me: I drive fast. The Florida state police have extravagant Christmas parties because of me.

Why would I do something so stupid? you might ask. Well, one person's stupid is another person's joy. I love it! I love the concentration it takes, the skill, and the sheer speed of it.

I love it so much, in fact, that I decided to take my need for speed to the racetrack and amp it up a bit. Fortunately, there's a three-step program for people like me, and it's called the Richard Petty Driving Experience. In this experience, you get behind the wheel of a NASCAR stock car and take eight laps at high speed around a professional racetrack. I found myself at the Homestead-Miami Speedway, which any NASCAR lover will tell you is a serious professional track.

Here are the steps: you pay, you train, you drive. You get about an hour of training, which consists of an introduction to the car, the track, and the flags. There are several flags you might get as you race around the track. The one I dreaded most was the rolled-up green flag, held snugly in the hand of the flagger and waved in a circular motion. It means, "Move it, slowpoke! Get your butt in gear!" I never saw this flag. I also didn't see the flag that told me I wasn't following my instructor closely enough. What I did get was a bunch of wave-offs from my instructor, meaning: "You're following too closely." A wave-off is good, because it means you're going the right speed. If you drop back just a bit, you're at the perfect distance for following.

"Four or five wave-offs is great," said our instructor, "because this shows you're not afraid of the speed, the track, or the car. Ten or eleven wave-offs probably means you have impulse control problems." I managed to control myself, but I can tell you that I wanted to go faster. I thought possibly that they were holding me back because I'm a girl, but more likely it had to do with their liability coverage. Even with the instructor controlling my speed, I drove at a top speed of 135 miles per hour and averaged about 120 around the track. (You have to slow down for those turns.)

I had also decided that I would ride as a passenger before I got behind the wheel myself. The professional driver I rode with took me right up to 165 miles per hour. He stayed on the wall, so close it seemed impossible that he wouldn't hit it and send us careening across the track in a fiery, out-of-control spin. It scared the pants off me. The track, the wall, and my life all passed before my eyes in a blur. I remember thinking to myself, "You want me to do *this?* What have I gotten myself *into?*" Maybe I should have taken the ride *after* I'd driven on the track myself, because it amped up my nerves about driving enormously.

But maybe not. The point of me getting behind the wheel of a stock car and driving it insanely fast was to laugh at my comfort zone, blow myself out of the envelope I live in, and expand my sense of possibilities. If I truly believe that I am a possibility amplifier, I have to act like one. Or rather, I *get* to act like one. I can throw off all the limitations that society, my brain, and my mother have imposed on me and drive as fast as I want. Well, as fast as the track's insurance company will let me.

So my question to you is, what are *you* doing to get yourself comfortable on the edge? What activities do you have planned for yourself for the specific purpose of increasing your risk tolerance? If you want to innovate your life, Risk Taking 101 is a prerequisite.

When I got off the track that night and headed home, I found myself driving my Acura 3.2 TL with a horrible case of lead foot combined with hysterical laughter. Luckily for me, no state or local police were in the immediate vicinity.

Racing a stock car and indoor skydiving might seem really

out there to you, and completely inaccessible given your current comfort zone. Maybe taking up a new sport, deciding to run a race, learning to scuba dive, or riding a Ferris wheel would be challenging and expanding for you. I encourage you to discover risks that challenge you without putting you in danger — not only physical risks but risks in other life categories as well. In part 2 of this book, you'll find plenty of examples of safe risk-taking that will open your heart and mind to more possibilities and help you make things happen.

Step 2. Supersize It, Please

Speaking of physical risk taking, if you watch the National Geographic or Discovery channels, you've probably seen Seth Warren and Tyler Bradt. They are extreme kayakers who have ridden some of the wildest rivers all over the world, and who are sponsored by kayak and outdoor gear companies. Now, that's a pretty big vision to have made come true, but for Seth and Tyler it wasn't big enough. They wanted the endless summer. An endless summer in water sports means that you follow the season around the globe, staying one step ahead of cold weather along the way. They had dreamed of such a trip, but they felt like they needed a better reason to go.

So, follow me here. First, they're taking enormous risks and having some of the most intense physical experiences of their lives in places all over the world — and getting somebody else to pay for it. But they decide they want more. So they take their dream to the next level and envision a straight year of kayaking and surfing. But that still isn't enough. They also want to combine their love of fast water with a philanthropic goal. Finally, they find the inspiration they need: a friend shows up driving a truck that runs on 100 percent vegetable oil. Their decision was instantaneous. They would spend their endless summer kayaking, surfing, and

— promoting biofuels. Seth and Tyler traveled from Alaska to the southern tip of Argentina without putting a drop of petroleum products in their biofuel-converted fire truck, educating communities about biofuels along the way. Oh, and then they made a movie of their adventure, which won multiple awards.[1]

Now *that's* a supersized vision.

You can supersize your aspirations as well. If you want to be as famous as Oprah Winfrey, imagine being *more* famous than Oprah. If you want a five-bedroom house on a lake with a maid to clean it all, imagine a ten-bedroom house on a *private* lake with a maid, a butler, and a chauffeur. If you want to be rich and work only four hours a day, imagine a business that makes you rich and lets you do anything you want all day long. The process of stretching the creative imagining of the vision you designed in chapter 1 will help you to expand your dream envelope to a size that encompasses much more of what the universe can really do for you.

Step 3. It's Not the Picture; It's the Frame

One of the tools the brain uses to organize information is *framing*. Your brain employs frames to sort and categorize your thoughts and experiences according to what you learned from your past experiences, right or wrong.

If mental frames were picture frames, and your thoughts and experiences were pictures, the brain would say, "Ah, this needs a four-by-six-inch frame, this one a three-by-five, and this one is wallet size," and would sort them accordingly. Of course, your mental frames are much more complex. The brain actually says something like, "Ah. This is a four-by-six-inch, red-hued, people-oriented picture taken in a foreign country called X, that happened in the year XXXX, during which time it was concluded that we would never vacation again with the Murpheys — or any other family for that matter, besides ours — and this type of picture goes with these types of pictures that are always framed in a gold, ornate, antique, wooden frame."

Mental frames make sense of complex information by giving it context or meaning. You have frames that describe and categorize the world, yourself, your spouse, your job, sex — everything. For example, when I say "Democrat," depending upon your own political beliefs you will have formed an image of "Democrat" in your mind that may or may not be complimentary. When you see a young girl with her midriff showing, you may look appreciatively or enviously at her toned, flat stomach, or think, "Tramp."

It's important to note that we make up these frames. It is we who decide how we will look at the world and categorize its contents. Other people may have helped to form our frames by providing input that we decided was important to include. For example, if your father was fond of saying that money doesn't grow on trees, you may have all kinds of scarcity frames around the concept of having money. If your (hopefully) former spouse repeatedly told you that you are an idiot, the mental frame through which you see yourself might include the idea that you're probably an idiot. But if your mother always told you, as mine did, that you were a bright girl and could be anything you ever wanted to be, then your frame for yourself will probably include the confidence that you can be anything you want to be. Your frames determine how you see situations, and they certainly limit or expand your capacity to see the available possibilities in those situations.

The crazy thing is that these frames are actually built into the physical structure of our brains. Since we use them repetitively, they become strong neural channels, meaning that the brain actually thickens and the neurons become more connected in those areas. That's why we find ourselves thinking the same things over and over again, even if we don't want to think them anymore.

The good news is that you can create new frames in your brain and establish new, strong neural connections. Called reframing, this is like removing a photograph from an old frame and placing it in a new, more modern frame. To do so, you must first identify the frame that is not serving you. For example, you may have a frame that says, "I am not destined to be wealthy." Discover the positive reasons behind your reason for having this frame in the first place. Keep in mind that some of your "positive" reasons could possibly be fabrications. For example, you may think, "By forgoing the possibility of wealth in my life, I will not have to learn about money management," or, "I don't want to work as hard as it takes to be wealthy."

Then, look at the positive reasons for dropping this frame and at the experience of life you could have if this frame did not exist. "If I believed I were destined to be wealthy, I could begin planning how to achieve that wealth and teach myself the principles of wealth management." "If I believed I were destined to be wealthy, I could start having more money now." If you can list any experiences you've had that negate the frame despite your belief in it, then review that list. For example, "I was recently given a promotion and raise, and expect another one soon."

Finally, design a new frame — a *reframed* idea — that will support the realization of your dream life. In this case it might be a belief such as: "I am destined to be wealthy, and becoming wealthy will be easy and fun."

Dr. Dean Ornish, a professor of medicine at the University of California, San Francisco, and founder of the Preventive Medicine Research Institute in Sausalito, California, knows the power of reframing. In his successful healthcare program, people with acute heart disease are taught a new way to look at their lives, thereby improving their health and avoiding heart surgery. And the changes stick.

How does he ask them to reframe their lives? Rather than terrifying them with the thought of their own potentially impending deaths, he invites them to create a new vision of how their lives could be if they rid themselves of the symptoms of their disease and their lives were pleasurable again. Thoughts about simple things like going to the store, walking the dog, or making love without experiencing pain have inspired his patients to stick with the program and avoid the operating table.

Some frames are not matters of life and death, but they still influence your ability to create the kind of life you want to live. For example, I once had a frame that said I would never win anything by chance, only by hard work. The positive reasons for having this frame were that it supported my belief that I am a hard worker and made me feel good about myself. My mother placed high importance on productivity, a value she passed to me. But I was pretty sure that if I did not have this frame, then I could widen my possibilities for bringing abundance into my life.

I looked back at my past to see if there was a time when I might have won something by chance. I remembered that when I was in elementary school, I attended a school jamboree. There I participated in a cakewalk, a simple game of chance played like musical chairs. The participants walk around a circle with numbers on it while the music plays. When the music stops, the organizer of the game calls out a number. Whoever is standing on that number wins a cake. I was on the correct number! I got to choose from a variety of delicious-looking cakes and pies and picked the biggest, most chocolaty cake I could find. I ran all the way home with it to show my mom. I remember being proud that I'd won that cake, even though there was no real skill involved. And I should have been, as it was the early me gladly accepting the abundance of the universe. *That* is the "me" I want to be.

My mental reframing of my old belief now states that the

universe is an abundant place, and I am constantly receiving unexpected — and unearned — gifts all the time. Every time I get
one, I tell my friends and family about it because, in that way, I
build up more experiential data that reinforces for my brain the
idea that the first frame was wrong and the new frame is right.

You may have a long list of frames that don't match up with
your amplified vision for yourself, but don't panic. Just design
your new frames and practice looking for the evidence that your
new frames are the right ones.

Keep your new frames simple, positive, and emotional. The
feelings, responses, and internal comments attached to your old
frames will still come up, but less and less frequently over time. In
those moments when they do, remind yourself of your new frame.
To continue with my earlier example, I would catch myself saying, "I never win anything by chance." The last time I said this, I
was holding a raffle ticket at a Thanksgiving luncheon. I looked
at my friends sitting around the table and said, "Well, that's
wrong, isn't it?" and promptly won a matching set of pilgrim salt
and pepper shakers. What a great way to break a frame!

Coincidentally, I also won an award for "best dessert" at that
luncheon, which reinforced my now slightly modified frame that
I *also* — not *only* — win things because of my own effort.

Releasing old frames will sometimes feel uncomfortable and
take courage. Often the people around you have as much invested
in your existing frames as you do. You may worry that they will
not understand if you begin to think and act differently because
you've chosen to reframe your experience.

It's okay. The interesting thing about change is that it often
triggers a "change back" response from those around you. I encourage you to hold tight to your dreams and create the frames that
support them, no matter what others may think. By practicing acceptance of your new frames, you will strengthen the connections

in your own brain and literally and physically change into the person of your dreams.

Step 4. Take Advantage of Your Superposition

The superposition principle of quantum physics states that when we do not know what the state of any object is, it is actually in all possible states simultaneously. In the moments before choosing, *you* are in a superposition in which all possibilities are available. The question is: What are they? As author C. Wright Mills once wrote, "Freedom is not merely the opportunity to do as one pleases; neither is it merely the opportunity to choose between set alternatives. Freedom is, first of all, *the chance to formulate the available choices*, to argue over them — and then, the opportunity to choose"[2] (italics mine).

One of the steps we often leave out when confronted with a decision to be made is adequately formulating our choices. Some of those choices seem ridiculous to us, so we pooh-pooh them when they show up in our awareness. Some are so scary that we avoid thinking about them because of the associated pain. Others are so far beyond our imagination machinery that they would never even occur to us. For example, there's a probability right at this moment that you might turn into a horse. Don't worry, it's a really, really tiny probability. But there are other possibilities out there with much higher probability that you are not considering. How can you bring those into your awareness?

That answer partly relies on whether an immediate decision is called for or you have some time to think it over. If an immediate decision is needed, here is the best advice I can ever give you: *pause*. More specifically, pause and *feel*. What feels right is what you should answer.

Too often our answers leap out of our mouths based on what we think we *should* say, rather than on what we really *want* to say.

Our habitual answers come out and trap us into things we don't want in our lives. That kind of choice ends up frustrating us, and frustration, I'm pretty sure, is not part of anyone's dream life.

When you have some time to think about your decision, first establish willingness to accept all the possibilities, even if some of them make you uncomfortable. (Just because they exist doesn't mean you have to choose them.) Then, map every possibility you can imagine. I like to use mind maps for this exercise, which you can draw freehand or with software. Mind maps are diagrams used to represent words, ideas, tasks, or other items linked to, and arranged around, a central keyword or idea. Visit www.Possibilities Amplified.com/resources.htm for some general information about the mind-mapping process and mind-mapping resources.

By its nature, mind mapping brings out possibilities that were invisible before. A mind map forces the person using it to take a holistic view of the situation being mapped and, as a result, often reveals new and unexpected answers. If you feel that you have captured every possibility you can think of, and still have not identified the right choice, it's time to look for more ideas. Here are some places you may find them:

- Business associates
- Internet sites for people going through similar situations
- Friends and family (Now, keep an open mind!)
- The bookstore, home of the latest and greatest thinking
- Support groups (There's one for everything out there.)
- Local seminars and workshops
- Experts (Call on them!)
- Magazines about unrelated topics (Reach outside the usual ones.)

These are just some of the places you can go to expand the pool of possibilities you choose from. By taking advantage of your superposition to adequately formulate your choices, you might find some seemingly outrageous and yet simply perfect possibilities, such as bravely borrowing money to start your own business, joyfully dropping a habit that's holding you back, or courageously pursuing a love relationship that nurtures and fulfills you.

Step 5. Tapping the Eureka Moment by Lying Down

You've been pounding away on a problem for hours or days that you just can't seem to nail down. No matter how you look at it, the answer still eludes you. Tired, you put the project aside and decide to lie down for a few minutes. Twenty minutes later, as you slowly return to consciousness, the answer to your problem appears perfectly formed in your mind. Your eyes fly open and you race back to your desk and double check to see whether this is the answer. Eureka! It is. And it came to you while you were sleeping.

Studies have demonstrated that taking breaks, particularly sleeping breaks, can reignite the creative process in the brain. Neuroendocrinologist Ullrich Wagner of the University of Luebeck in Germany conducted a study in 2004 in which subjects were presented with stimulus-response sequences and were expected to improve their response speed over time. The subjects were told that there was also a hidden, abstract rule underlying the sequences that would allow them to improve their times dramatically. All subjects were given a break before they found the hidden rule. Some slept and some did not, and then they all returned to the task. More than twice as many of the subjects who slept discovered the hidden rule, compared to those who did not sleep. Wagner attributes this to a process of memory restructuring and reconsolidation that takes place during sleep.

Whatever the mechanism, if you confront an obstacle in your

attempts to amplify possibility, you might want to lie down and think about your topic for a bit. Coincidentally, researchers have also discovered that taking naps reduces your chance of having a heart attack. So I'm serious about this: take a nap.

Step 6. Focus on Your Strengths

We spend a lot of time worrying about our weaknesses, trying to shore up our defenses against them, and trying to round ourselves out by fixing those weaknesses. All this time and energy is wasted. You have a set of strengths, and you will get much better results, much faster, and be much more fulfilled by focusing on using those strengths than you ever will by focusing on fixing your weaknesses.

These were the findings of the authors of *Now, Discover Your Strengths*, Marcus Buckingham and Donald O. Clifton. This book represents the analysis of over two million interviews with professionals conducted by the Gallup Organization. Thirty-four strength themes were culled from those interviews. In *Now, Discover Your Strengths 2.0* by Tom Rath, it becomes apparent how deeply ingrained the philosophy of fixing weaknesses really is. Let's say your child comes home with a report card showing As and Bs and one F. Which grade are you most likely to focus on? Seventy-seven percent of parents in the United States would focus on the F. As Rath states, parents and teachers greet excellence with apathy and spend enormous amounts of time and attention on a child's lowest grades.

How is that likely to play out for the child? The child is likely to feel that her successful efforts are unappreciated. She might come to like school less, since she can't get adequate positive feedback on the things she does there very well. She might even become less productive at school, since apparently her good performance doesn't really make much difference to the authority figures and mentors in her life.

This is not just about children. A similar pattern is playing out across corporate America. Employees who do work that does not use their strengths are less engaged, less fulfilled, and more likely to leave their companies than those whose work does use their strengths. You may know how it feels at home when you're constantly being called on the carpet for the negative things you've done and seldom celebrated for the things you've done right. Employees feel the same way on the job.

If you have been trying to fix yourself, you're probably much clearer on your weaknesses than you are on your strengths. It may be easy for you to list five of your strengths, but can you list your top five? Can you list the five that will make the most difference to the creation of your dreams? I sure couldn't. It wasn't until I read *Now, Discover Your Strengths* that I developed a firm picture of what my top strengths are and really began to leverage them in my life.

Now, Discover Your Strengths is one tool you can use to find out more about yourself. You can also try the Myers-Briggs personality inventory test, based on the theories of Carl Jung. This test will peg you as a certain "type" regarding the way you think, intuit, sense, and feel. At the time of this writing, several free and interesting self-evaluation tools could be found online. Type "free personality test" into your favorite online search engine to find those that are available today. Lastly, you might consider performing a personal SWOT analysis.

SWOT stands for strengths, weaknesses, opportunities, and threats. The SWOT analysis is usually applied to businesses but has the same value when applied personally. In this analysis, you attempt to identify and list your own strengths and weaknesses, but you also define opportunities available to you because of your uniqueness, such as a promotion, or your ability to shape the thoughts of others by telling your personal experiences. Similarly, you identify potential threats to your success, such as a changing work environment, an emotionally distant spouse, or addictive behaviors. The cool thing about the SWOT is that it puts your possible future scenarios (your opportunities and threats) and the tools you have to shape them (your strengths and weaknesses) on a single page, from which ideas will begin to flow.

Step 7. Go Ahead, Cry (for Joy)

I've learned from my coaching and consulting practices that when most people design a vision of a dream future, they think about and write down all the things or experiences they believe will make them happy, such as a car, a second home, a trip to Europe, or a raise. But they don't write down "feel happy," even though it is their emotional state they're trying to fix most.

If you think adding some money to your life is the key to happiness, I'm sure you've heard the saying about how much happiness money can buy. (None.) A 2006 study by a couple of Princeton professors, economist Alan B. Krueger and psychologist and Nobel laureate Daniel Kahneman, found that once the rent or mortgage is covered, money is less significant to happiness than predicted, and that people with higher incomes do not necessarily spend more time in enjoyable ways.

Krueger and Kahneman's study looked at people's overall life satisfaction as well as their moment-to-moment experience, and it revealed that income is just not that important in the moment-to-moment experience of life. Study participants rated the different types of experiences they had throughout the day, and among those they rated the highest was socializing. So, one way to practice being happy is to spend a lot of time hanging out with your friends. People with lower incomes gave themselves permission more often to do this. If you get rich, will you give yourself permission to just hang out with your friends? Are you giving yourself permission now?

If you really want to change the way you feel, you have to prioritize what's important to you. Here's why. Whatever emotions you are practicing now will continue to be the emotions you practice in the future — no matter what that future looks like — unless you decide you want to change them and start practicing the emotions you want. Yes, I'm talking about practicing happiness.

Here are a couple of my favorite emotions to practice: frustration and worry. I am really good at these emotions. I have practiced and practiced and practiced them. The emotions I wish I had practiced more are lightheartedness, gratefulness, and patience, and I'm consciously practicing those now and getting better at them. What emotions are you practicing? What emotions would you like to start practicing?

Happiness is not going to leap out of a cake and surprise you today or any time in the future. Happiness is a choice. If you want to get a head start on crafting the emotional life that will support your dream life, I recommend Lynn Grabhorn's book, *Excuse Me, Your Life Is Waiting: The Astonishing Power of Feelings*. You can find this great book and others like it on my website.

Step 8. Wake Up: You Bought a Home in Mudslide Central

Perhaps you didn't know when you bought the house — or accepted the promotion, or married the person — that you had just made an investment in a well-known mudslide zone. Or maybe you did. But maybe you thought that *your* house was on stable ground, that *your* house would be an exception. But here's the truth: There ain't none. A mudslide zone is a mudslide zone, and your house will end up at the mucky bottom sooner or later.

So let's just say you didn't know. Or let's say that you had some evidence, but you decided to ignore it because you loved the house so much. Or perhaps you had some evidence but also felt you had no choice. In any case, there you find yourself, living in the middle of Mudslide Central.

One day, the house shudders a bit. You grab the edges of the breakfast table, but nothing else happens, and so you go on with your day, thinking, "Surely that was just a little nothing." Then one night, your bed tilts sideways and you're thrown on the floor. As you lie with your face in the carpet, nothing else happens, so you get back in your tilting bed and fall asleep as best you can. The next morning, you call the foundation repair people, and you go on with your day, thinking, "Surely a little foundation repair will clear this right up."

Never once do you allow yourself to think, "*My house is about to slide down a hill, to be wrecked forever.*" Because what would that mean? It would mean that the worst possible outcome to this little slippage problem actually could happen. If we are good at anything, we are good at denial. It's almost as if we think denial can overcome gravity. But allowing fear of the worst possible outcome to run our lives is sometimes more painful than the worst possible outcome itself.

Bob Parsons is the CEO of the amazingly popular website GoDaddy.com, the largest accredited registrar of Internet domain names in the United States. (You may have seen their controversial Super Bowl ads.) Bob was only eighteen when he was assigned to a rifle squad in Vietnam. He was terribly afraid, lacked experience, and longed to see his family and home once again. On his first day as a replacement for a dead Marine, Bob worked himself into a panic attack thinking about the insurmountable odds facing him. He was barely able to function.

Then a realization hit him: he was meant to die in Vietnam. He could not imagine a way in which he would escape with his life. With that realization, a deep calm came over him. By accepting that worst possible outcome, Bob was able to function again, successfully fulfilled his duty, and came home alive. *By accepting the worst possible outcome, Bob freed his mind.* Likewise, by accepting the possibility that your Mudslide Central home will end up at the mucky bottom, you can free your mind to consider all the possibilities that surround that inevitable event.

Fear of the worst possible outcome can be a major internal roadblock to the amplification process. By having the courage to accept and integrate the worst outcome we can imagine, even in the most difficult of circumstances, we take back our right to choose our response. In that choice, we can begin the creation process all over again and find the fuel we need to press on.

Step 9. Quantum Tunnel It

Subatomic particles are able to tunnel through barriers that should be impassable according to the rules of classical (nonquantum) physics. Virtually every time quantum tunneling is mentioned in books or online, the metaphor of rolling a ball up and over a hill is used. Tunneling occurs when there's not enough energy to get the ball over the top of the hill and yet the quantum ball can still be found on the other side of the metaphorical hill. Quantum particles can do this because they have the properties of waves. As you now know from chapter 1, in wave form a subatomic particle can be everywhere at once, so being on the other side of the hill is not such a big deal.

The same is true of you when you are up against an obstacle. In particle mode, you will find the obstacle impenetrable. You'll know you're in particle mode when you believe there's only one right answer to the problem before you, and your frustration and disbelief are mounting. By tapping into your wave mode, however, you will find yourself magically on the other side of the obstacle.

Here's how I think it works:

1. Accept that the answer you are striving for is only one of an infinite set of possibilities.
2. Release your answer, because while you're holding on to it you're still in particle mode.
3. Ask the universe to deliver the best possible solution it can provide.
4. Create a mindset of expectant anticipation that the solution will be delivered.
5. To solidify your own belief about the outcome, you can try some of what I call "pre-thanking" — expressing gratitude for the as-yet-undelivered answer.
6. Stand back.

While you are waiting, you might try being even more wave-y by considering some of the ways the universe might meet your request and imagining your response to each option. If, while you're waiting, you hit upon a solution that you think will work, well, by all means, implement away. The important thing is to keep moving.

We often hit obstacles when we're dealing with other people, because, guess what, other people have visions and dreams too, and their dreams don't always match up perfectly with ours. The method that has always worked best for me when my vision is at odds with the vision of another is to try to help the other person realize his or her vision while at the same time I realize mine. To do this, you'll need to ask the other person what he needs or wants from the situation, express what you need or want, and then together craft a solution that can make both your visions happen simultaneously.

Step 10. "Re-Memorying" the Past

Most of us have three big pictures of the future: one that looks kind of like a continuation of the present we believe we are experiencing today, one that looks like our worst nightmare, and one in which our dreams come true. In the first two cases, we say things like: "I can't do anything about my life until the kids go away to college; then I'll be able to do that traveling I've wanted to do, or start my own business," or whatever, thereby keeping life exactly the way it is, and our dreams just dreams.

Or: "I couldn't possibly take that internship in Australia; the kids are in college and they still need me. I can't be halfway around the world, because what if something goes wrong?" Then we imagine our children in the hospital and the twenty-four hours it will take for us to get there, however unlikely it is that this will happen. Or we may say, "If I quit my job now, what will I do about all these bills?" (Go bankrupt, probably.) Or: "I'd really like a partner, but I'm so sick of dating, and I never meet the right one, and maybe something's wrong with me that I'll never be able to fix," and so on.

We imagine that our interpretations of the events occurring in this universe — and the ones we are making up about the future — are the truth. They are, in fact, our creations, and we are choosing them all the time.

At the same time, we can envision a dream life, a universe in which we achieve greatness, or finally get to relax, or get to travel, or meet the man or woman of our dreams and fall in love, or maybe all of the above, and in our current state, that state seems foreign. It seems virtually impossible.

But, I can guarantee you that if you've wanted this dream for a long time, then you have already created some history that will enable it to occur. Recognize that history, observe it, learn from it, and you're on your way.

Instead of remembering your past in the traditional way, you can "re-memory" it, culling events that point in the direction of your dreams. Let me use a piece of my own re-memory as an example. Part of my dream life included being the author of a book.

As you can see, that vision has come true. I didn't always think it was actually possible, though, since I'd started several books and hadn't finished any of them. In fact, my past performance nearly had me convinced that I couldn't do it. So I reached back into my past and re-memoried it.

Here's part of my newly crafted past that supports my ability to write a book:

During my senior year of high school, I won a school board essay-writing contest and appeared on public television.

As an adult, I wrote an article on productivity that was published in a computer magazine. For a small, biweekly business newspaper for which I served as a technology consultant, I wrote an article on the illegal export of computers. The editor told me that it required less editing than pieces by some of her professional reporters. They published it.

While on a consulting engagement at the *Miami Herald*, I got to meet the staff of the *Herald*'s then-Sunday magazine, *Tropic*, which I loved. One day, I bravely walked in and handed the editor an essay I had written for the magazine's "Can't Live without 'Em" column. He called me a few days later to say he wanted to buy it. I was paid to write! I was now a professional writer. I published many more essays in *Tropic* over the next couple of years.

Tropic magazine later bought a fiction piece from me, making me a professional fiction writer.

A friend of mine, a previous boss and a many-times-published book author, Janine Warner, asked if I would like to contribute to a "Dummies" book she was writing. You know, those yellow-and-black books you see all the time in the bookstore? How could I say no? I wrote a few chapters of that book, *Managing Web Projects for Dummies*. Now I had my name, bio, and picture in a published book with a fabulous brand name, even if I was not on the cover. I was getting closer.

I wrote and published a book called *The Science of Making Things Happen: Turn Any Possibility into Reality.*

What's just as important as finding these contributory events in your past is understanding what you learned from each event. Follow the path of knowledge and you'll end up at the door of your dream life.

What I learned from the high school essay contest, for example, was that other people are interested in my success and want to help me access the potentiality of the universe. My honors semantics teacher entered my paper in that contest. Now I know I need to seek and accept the help of my supporters. I don't have to do it alone. From that experience I also learned that I am confident being on camera and talking about my work.

As an article and essay writer, I discovered that despite not having any formal training as a writer, I'm as good a writer as some who have received such training. That bolstered my confidence and my continued belief in my dream. By being published as a contributor to *Managing Web Projects for Dummies*, I began to glimpse the inside world of book writing and publishing, a glimpse that would turn into years of additional learning.

There are all kinds of tools you can use to re-memory your past. I'm fond of journaling for this task, but you can record your re-memories on audio or video. You can become the storyteller of your re-memoried past and share your story with your family and friends. You can create a mind map of your re-memories. You can even draw them. Choose the modality that resonates with you the most, and review your re-memory often.

Step 11. Question Authority

Imagine this. You have responded to an ad in the newspaper asking for participants in a study at Yale University. Respondents will receive twenty dollars. You sign up and arrive at the designated place on campus. There you are greeted by a stern-looking biology professor in a white lab coat and introduced to another participant. The professor explains that this is an experiment to test the effects of punishment on learning. One participant will be the teacher, the other the learner. You are asked to pick a piece of paper from a bowl. Your slip of paper says "teacher." The other participant draws "learner."

The biology professor explains that as the teacher, you will be given a list of word pairs to teach to the learner. You will read the list of pairs first, then test the learner's recall using multiple-choice questions. For each wrong answer, you are to push a switch that will shock the learner. You are given a sample of the shock. You are also told that with each wrong answer, the voltage of the shock will increase. The learner goes into the next room.

The learner is apparently very slow, because he gets a lot of wrong answers. You find yourself administering stronger and stronger shocks, with encouragement from the professor when you find yourself faltering. You can hear the learner's shouts, then screams of pain coming from the next room, and as the voltage increases, he begins to bang on the wall. At some point, the learner yells out that he has a heart condition. Then, after one particularly loud scream, the learner no longer responds to your questions. You want to check on the learner, but the professor asks you to continue. You object. He insists that you continue. You still are not sure and are feeling stressed besides. He says that it is imperative that the experiment be completed, and that you have no choice but to continue.

Do you?

Here's the "shocking" answer. Most of us would. In this real study, conducted in 1961 at Yale University by psychologist Stanley Milgram, 65 percent of participants administered the final 450-volt shock. (No actual shocks were being administered to the actor "learners," but the situation appeared real to the "teacher" participants.) It didn't matter if the participants were uneducated or had doctorates. It didn't matter if they were poor or well off. It didn't matter if they were male or female. It didn't matter that they were undergoing extreme emotional distress during the experiment. No matter who they were, they felt compelled to obey the authority figure in the white lab coat.

Sometimes participants were joined by one or more other "teachers," actors who pretended to have been recruited too. Whether or not the peer teacher refused or agreed to comply, the vast majority of participants went along with the peer teacher's choice. In other words, not only were participants almost helpless against authority, but they also were persuaded by the behavior of their peers, even when it meant the participants were breaching their own moral standards.

I'd love to tell you that since this study was done in the 1960s we've evolved into more independent beings. Unfortunately, more recent studies and news events indicate otherwise. Ten years after the Milgram experiments were conducted, Leonard Bickman of Smith College conducted a study to determine the effect of a uniform in inducing compliance, which was published in the *Journal of Applied Social Psychology*.[3] Subjects in the study were stopped in the street by someone dressed as either a civilian, a milkman, or a guard and asked to perform certain actions. The subjects were more likely to obey the guard — the man in the uniform of a perceived legitimate authority — than the others. Whether it's a white lab coat or a uniform, the symbols of authority are all around you and have the power to influence your choices from moment to moment.

You may have heard of the Strip Search Prank Call Scam, a series of hoax calls that went on for about a decade, until 2004. Targeting fast-food restaurants in over seventy incidents, a man claiming to be a police officer convinced store managers to strip-search female employees *and customers.* The managers, their employees, and even the women's significant others went to extraordinary lengths to obey the unknown man on the phone — including conducting body cavity searches, spanking, and otherwise humiliating these women — *because they thought he represented authority.*[4] What authority figures might you be giving your power away to?

If you want to amp up the vision of your dream future and protect its integrity, include the values that you will hold firm to and don't let anyone sway you from them. If you have already given some of yourself away in order to avoid conflict, or because you were unsure of your own voice, or for any other reason, I encourage you to take yourself back. Fight to be who you are, so that when you find yourself in your dream life, you will love the person you spend most of your time with — yourself.

Step 12. Cary Grant It

If, like Archibald Leach, you act as though you are a smooth and debonair movie star, you soon will be. Archibald Leach was born in Bristol, England, in 1904 to a poor family. His mother had a nervous breakdown when he was nine (supposedly, although accounts conflict as to whether his two-timing alcoholic father might have made that up), and she was committed to a mental institution. Archie's father told him that his mother had abandoned them, thinking that a better explanation. At fourteen, Archie ran away from home, joined the circus, and ended up in the United States. The circus eventually led to the stage, and the stage led to the big screen.

When he was twenty-seven years old, Paramount Pictures renamed him Cary Grant, and that's what he would be called for the rest of his life. But the soul of Cary Grant existed long before that. Cary Grant was a persona that Archie crafted from his own personal experiences and observations. He designed the person he wanted to be and then became him. As Grant put it, "I pretended to be somebody I wanted to be until finally I became that person. Or he became me."

Nobody who ever watched a Cary Grant movie would say that Archibald Leach failed at what he set out to do. His wit, humor, comedic timing, and physical elegance put him in a class all by himself. In his career and life, there was a point at which Archie Leach was assimilated completely by Cary Grant, and at that point all of Archie's past merged with his desires for the future, so that *he became his desires*. His career took off, and more important, he took control of his career. He negotiated terms for his contracts the likes of which had never before been seen in Hollywood, and he became a model for the free agent concept. He did only movies in which he would shine. Cary Grant had come into himself, and it was a self he had made up.

I invite you to create your own persona. When you look at the vision you have created for yourself, is there a clear picture of who you will be in that vision? Are you a confident entrepreneur? A laid-back billionaire? A sexy model type? An athletic powerhouse? Maybe you're someone who doesn't live at Mom's house anymore. Whatever your vision of yourself in your dream life, try the following exercise.

1. Wake up in the morning. Replace the thoughts that habitually come to you at this time with the thoughts of the person you have planned to be. I think you'll find they cheer you up right away.

2. Experience the day as your Cary Grant. Whatever you have named the "you" in your dream life (and I do hope you have chosen a name; it's okay if it's your regular name, but maybe put *Super* in front of it),

wear your vision like a skin all day. Respond to situations as if you were the new you. Answer emails, conduct phone conversations, and interact with family, friends, colleagues, and associates as if you were the "you" of your dreams. Even conduct your alone time as if you were this person. Because guess what? You are! Archibald Leach always had Cary Grant inside him.

And if you haven't created your new persona yet, do that now. Know who you want to be, and how you want to feel, and who you will no longer worry about being anymore. Discard the directives from your mom and your dad, your boss, and all the other people who told you who you need to be in order to succeed. You get to decide. Decide well, my possibility-amplifying friend.

3. EPIGENETICS

Changing Yourself Is an Outside Job

IN 2005, A FRENCH ARTIST NAMED RODOLPHE GOMBERGH exhibited a collection of artworks in Paris that combined new technology and ancient tradition. Called Hidden Treasures: The Inner Life of the Buddhas, the exhibit consisted of CT scans — more familiarly known as CAT scans — of Korean Buddha statues dating from the eleventh century to the eighteenth century. Inside the Buddhas, the CT scans revealed, were hidden pearls, strands of jewels, sacred texts, and messages.[1]

When the artists who carved and built the statues stored secret treasures inside them, what were they hoping to accomplish? Perhaps they were safeguarding the wealth of their families and country from invaders. By adding sacred texts, they may have further sanctified the gilded symbols of their religion. If they gave these statues as gifts, were they able to pass secret messages to their allies in times of strife? It's entirely possible that the statue designers wanted only to create objects that were beautiful and worthy of appreciation both inside and out. I can most assuredly say that you are a person who has these characteristics as well.

The purpose of this chapter is to share with you the reasons for paying attention to your own internal environment. Just as the CT scan is a new and revealing way to look at an object carved of wood, this chapter will provide you with a new way to think of yourself and the internal world you are creating in each moment. The truth is, your belief system can turn lead into gold if you will take responsibility for governing it. What hidden treasures are waiting inside you?

THE POWER OF EPIGENETICS

"I can't help it. It's in my genes."

If you've ever uttered these words, I have some news for you: just because it's in there, doesn't mean you can't get it out. To best explain why you have the power to override your DNA, let's start with mice.

Just like humans, not all mice are born normal. Some are born with genetic predispositions to various maladies and syndromes. One such mouse is now popularly known as the agouti mouse, and an experiment conducted with this type of mouse was featured on the cover of virtually every science magazine on the newsstands at the end of 2006.

This mouse carries a mutant form of the agouti gene, which is responsible for fur color. In its most lethal form, this gene mutation causes — in your typical brown mouse — a yellow coat, diabetes, obesity, and tumors. The mutation is 100 percent hereditary.

In the experiment, scientists discovered that if they fed a specific diet to a pregnant mouse with this gene mutation, the baby mice would be born without the yellow coat and physical defects associated with it. The baby mice still carried the gene mutation, but its effects were switched off. In other words, the *environment* the baby mice experienced while in the womb overcame their genes.

The increasingly exciting field of epigenetics is the study of forces that modify the way genes express themselves without modifying the genes themselves. Until very recently, it was thought that once your DNA was encoded in early development, that was it. You were stuck with it. But now it has become apparent that it's possible for us to change the way our genes express themselves during our lifetimes. Randy Jirtle, a professor of radiation oncology at Duke University and one of the designers of the agouti mouse experiment, says that "epigenetics introduces the concept of free will into our idea of genetics."[2]

In fact, some changes in gene expression are probably designed to happen during a being's lifetime. For example, Michael J. Meaney, director of the McGill Centre for the Study of Behaviour, Genes and Environment in Montreal was able to trace brain changes in rats to the nurturing behavior of their mothers. Rats that were licked and groomed more by their mothers were braver and calmer than rats neglected by their moms, which developed skittish and fearful behavior. Meaney discovered that the brains of well-nurtured rats differed from those of their neglected counterparts: their hippocampi were bigger and better developed. Less of a stress hormone called cortisol was produced in their bodies.

It has been suggested that this change in gene expression was designed to happen after baby rats are born so that rat mothers can fine-tune their babies' behavior and help them survive the environment into which they have been born. Meaney is now exploring whether the same sort of development opportunities exist for human babies as well. The "nature versus nurture" argument about child rearing takes on a different light in this context. It appears that behavior is the result of both.

These new discoveries fly in the face of conventional biology. It has always been thought that the silencing or activation of gene expression occurs only in embryonic or fetal cells, not in the mature cells of a child or adult. Now we know that even when we are adults, the environment in which we find ourselves *or create for ourselves* has a biological impact at the cellular level.

Every day, you are dealing with two environments: the one that surrounds you and the one that exists within your own body. Dr. Bruce Lipton, a cell biologist and the author of *The Biology of Belief*, in his book eloquently describes the impact that environment has on every cell in our body. The nucleus — which contains the cell's genetic material — is not the "brain" of the cell after all, Lipton says. The cell membrane is in charge. Everything the cell does reflects what it comes in contact with in its environment. The membrane is covered with a collection of protein receptors and sensors designed to perceive and connect with components critical to the cell and to reject substances that will harm it. Examples of these components include hormones, neurotransmitters, and cytokines — all signaling substances that our bodies generate — and nutrition, such as glucose. Toxins like bacteria are rejected. The sensors in the cell membrane respond not only to physical molecules but to energy fields as well. There are also effector proteins on the cell membrane. These proteins decide how the cell will respond to the myriad stimuli it receives. So even at the cellular level, we are engaged in a process of observation, awareness, and action.

Given a healthy and safe environment, the cell will properly take in or turn away substances and perform optimally. Unfortunately, our cells are not always in a healthy and safe environment. Our brains sometimes send down signals that the cell has no choice but to receive and obey.

Putting aside for a moment health risks such as obesity, smoking, excessive drinking, drug use, sedentary lifestyle, and so on, let's look at one particular cause for much of the cell's woes: fear. Or in today's jargon, stress.

Your body has basically two modes: growth and protection. When your body is in growth mode, it's in a creation process, building what it needs to maintain and renew itself. Your cells are actively reproducing, taking in nutrients, creating new proteins, and so on. When your body is in protection mode, your cells are inhibited from expending energy on growth, because the body re-purposes that energy for survival.

Whereas our ancestors were afraid of being eaten by cougars and the like, and often had to fight or run away to save themselves, we have a much longer list of threats and can't physically fight or run away in order to escape them. We're afraid of losing our jobs, of making our kids' lives a mess, of our bad behaviors being dis-covered, of not being good enough, of looking like idiots, of not being able to take care of our families, of losing our significant oth-ers, of not finding significant others, of not having enough money to retire. And, as if these fears and others like them were not enough, we have the advertising industry reminding us that we should be afraid of heartburn, that we don't have the right cars, that we sweat too much, that our houses smell, that our teeth aren't white enough, that our hair isn't silky, that our noses are too big, and that we won't know when it's the right time for that first Botox injection.

Women in particular are bombarded with new worries daily. I personally have a voice in my head that reminds me of all the rules I have absorbed over the years from beauty magazines. When I wash my hair, this voice often pops up to remind me of the article I read on how you're not supposed to put shampoo directly on the roots, because it makes your hair look flat. The voice re-minds me that I'm not supposed to pluck above my eyebrows, only below, and that I should use only my ring finger to apply cream in the under-eye area because it's so delicate, apparently, that I'm likely to rub it off.

And if you're a single mom with young kids in daycare and a career, I know you've had that panic attack when you realize that traffic is much worse than you anticipated, and that you will be late picking up your children *again*. (Probably marring them for life in the process, and forever labeling you as a "bad mom" in the minds of the daycare workers.)

As we go through our days measuring ourselves against an infinite landscape of yardsticks, our panic button gets hit again and again. The brain, in order to help us escape all these threats, sends signals to the body to release adrenaline and cortisol, the hormones designed to save us from being eaten by cougars. As you might imagine, they're powerful chemicals. Pumping them into the system regularly not only damages the body but also changes it, making it easier and easier to turn on the stress response. "If I'm in this much danger," the brain thinks, "I'd better open up the channels a little bit." And soon you're operating at a hopped-up level well above where you should be, dealing with sleep problems, feeling fatigued, and having almost completely forgotten how to have fun.

Your cells have forgotten, too. When your cells receive these hormonal signals, they change their configuration. They stop their happy labor and start conserving energy. If your immune system is in the middle of fighting an infection, it stops, because all of the body's energy is being diverted to saving your ass from the huge threat (child sick at school again/boss on a rampage/fender bender at Toys-R-Us) looming on the horizon. And we wonder why our gums hurt and our wounds won't heal and our allergies kick up. There's only so much energy in the system, and as a result it's impossible for the body to support both the growth mode and the protection mode at the same time.

Given that your goal is now to amplify your dream life into reality, where will you get the energy for that? It's clear that when your body is in protection mode, it will not be able to support your creation process in an optimum way, or even at all. So the trick is to keep your body in growth mode and then stoke the system to produce maximum energy.

YOUR BELIEFS:
THE CORNERSTONE OF GROWTH MODE

The triggers that cause your body to produce a stress response are purely the result of your *perception* of them as a threat. Each of us is living in a world of our own design and based on our perception of reality. We have beliefs about who we are and how the world works. Some of these beliefs are factual, and some of them are based on information we've received during our lifetimes that is not true. One of my favorite ways to illustrate this is a *Calvin and Hobbes* cartoon. Calvin is a little boy, and Hobbes is his stuffed tiger who comes to life in Calvin's mind. In this cartoon, Calvin's dad provides us with an example of how parents embed false beliefs in their children.

I wonder how old Calvin gets to be before he realizes that his dad was full of it? I remember my dad telling my sister and me, when we wondered where all the dark storm clouds had gone, that dirty clouds go to Pittsburgh to get cleaned. Dads are notorious for spreading this kind of stuff.

But remember, even mom joined in and told you there was a Santa Claus, an Easter Bunny, and a Tooth Fairy. Do you remember when these fictions were finally revealed to you? Do you think it's possible that you've got some other beliefs that are about as true as the Easter Bunny? For example, your father may have told you that you'll never amount to anything. Or your mother might have told you that ladies always keep their legs crossed. You may have learned that the world is a place of scarcity and want. You might believe that all men or all women can't be trusted. How much of your belief system is composed of things you can actually prove or disprove? How much of your belief system serves you in positive ways? How much of your belief system have you actually examined and mapped? The answers to these questions are critically important to the successful amplification of your vision into reality.

YOUR BELIEF MANAGEMENT SYSTEM

Some say that when two people come together in a relationship, they become one. I say they become three: the two individuals and the relationship. The relationship is a third entity that needs to be nurtured, examined, cared for, and managed. In business, a similar structure exists: there's a process that will get a certain function done, and then there's the process management system.

In either case, the questions are these: What are we trying to make happen here? Is this relationship/process working the way we want it to work? How will we know? What are the methods available to us for fixing it? What's the contingency plan if things should go awry? What agreement/documentation is in place? Is the agreement/documentation being followed? Are all the right resources available? Is there a place where the process/relationship always gets hung up? How does this process/relationship fit in with the other processes/relationships that might exist and come in contact with it? When will we know if the process/relationship is outdated and needs to be dismantled or replaced? (That last one always makes me laugh. Generally we don't go into relationships with a plan for getting out, but maybe we should, and not just financially.)

A management system gives participants and managers (and in relationships, consider yourself both a participant and a manager) an expanded view that would otherwise not be available.

Your beliefs need a management system, too, because — and here's a newsflash — your unexamined beliefs are running your life. You operate in accordance with them whether you know what they are or not. Imagine the woman who dates unavailable men over and over again because deep inside she believes that if she can just get one of them to love her the way she wants, she will finally prove she's lovable. Imagine the man who lashes out with his fists whenever his manhood is questioned, because each time he does so he proves that his father was wrong about his boyhood self being a weakling. Your beliefs can even lead you to assign values or character traits to others that they don't necessarily have, and then to make up reasons for their actions.

But it's not all doom and gloom. Your beliefs can powerfully work to your advantage as well. They can lift depression and relieve physical ailments. Your beliefs can make you healthier. Harvard University researchers recently did a study in which they informed certain hotel housekeepers that their daily work was sufficient to keep them fit. A control group of other housekeepers was told nothing. Four weeks later, the researchers returned to discover that the informed housekeepers had lost an average of two pounds, had lowered their blood pressure by almost 10 percent, and had made meaningful reductions in body mass index, compared to the control group. In only four weeks. They believed they were fit, and their beliefs literally reshaped them.

You may not know this, but for years doctors have been performing fake surgeries — also known as placebo-controlled surgical trials — on their patients. In 2002, a study by the Baylor College of Medicine revealed that patients with osteoarthritis of the knee were made to believe that they were receiving arthroscopic surgery, when in fact just a tiny incision was made. Throughout the postsurgical observation period, the patients who received fake surgery reported results even better than those reported by the patients who had the real surgery.

In July of 2007, researchers at Columbia University discovered that the brain actually released more natural painkillers, called opioids, when test volunteers who thought a painkiller had been applied to their forearms received a painful stimulus there. Further, their *expectation* of how well the topically applied "painkiller" would work correlated with how much of the natural painkiller was released by the brain. Positive expectations caused the brain to produce a chemical reaction.

In 2002, a study conducted by Dr. Andrew Leuchter, director of adult psychiatry at the UCLA Neuropsychiatric Institute, demonstrated that patients suffering from depression who received a placebo instead of an antidepressant drug achieved the same level of relief from symptoms as those on the drug. Thirty-eight percent of the patients given the placebo responded to treatment, compared to 52 percent of those receiving the antidepressant. At the eight-week mark, you could not tell the difference between the two responding groups, except for one telltale sign: those taking the drug showed suppressed activity in the prefrontal part of the brain, whereas those receiving the placebo showed *more* activity. *Their brains were working on their behalf to make their beliefs come true.*

After eight weeks, the patients on the placebo were told that they were on a placebo. Without exception, all of them slipped back into a depressed state, losing the improvements they had gained.

POSSIBILITY TIP

Basing your beliefs on other people or on events outside your control leaves you more open to the disruption of those beliefs. If you believe that your marriage will not fail because your spouse loves you, you are more likely to have that belief shattered than if you believe your marriage will succeed because you are committed to doing anything it takes to keep it fresh and make it work. Your spouse may still find a reason to leave, but if you have been conducting yourself according to your belief about your commitment, you will know that you did everything you could at your end.

Your beliefs alone can create or sabotage the internal environment necessary to make your dreams come true. This means that identifying and managing your beliefs is the way to stay in growth mode much more of the time, and spending time practicing the beliefs that serve you is the way to maximize your available energy.

To establish your belief management system, follow these simple steps:

1. Identify your current beliefs about yourself and the world.
2. Identify the beliefs that do not serve the amplification of your vision into reality, and those that do.
3. Replace the negative beliefs with positive ones that *do* support your amplification process.
4. Practice your new collection of positive beliefs.

5. Modify your belief system as necessary to fine-tune your results.

Do all these steps in writing. The management process becomes much easier and will be cause for less debate with yourself when you have adequate documentation. Take time alone to think through your beliefs and record what comes up.

Once you begin paying attention to your beliefs, you will start to notice behaviors of your own that you can't quite explain. "Why did I say that?" you might ask yourself. You'll question the belief motivation behind it. You'll be astonished at the personal beliefs you uncover just by observing your own behavior. You can add these beliefs to your belief management system and keep them or replace them, depending upon how well they serve you. Again, awareness creates change.

A QUANTUM LEAP OF FAITH

You may be saying to yourself: "You can't change your beliefs just like that!" And you'd be right. There are two more things you'll need to do if you truly wish to modify your belief system: Make the decision to do so. And then put your attention on it.

One of the beautiful aspects of the Possibility Amplification Process is that it not only amplifies into reality the things and experiences you want, but it also amplifies a new and more powerful *you* into reality. When you truly take responsibility for your role as the creator of your universe, as a master of the energy and space around you, as the best-designed possibility amplifier in the universe, you re-create yourself along with everything else. Your personal transformation is part of the deal.

Michael Merzenich, faculty member and researcher in the Department of Otolaryngology at the University of California, San Francisco, wrote with a colleague that through attention, "we choose and sculpt how our ever-changing minds will work, we choose who we will be in the next moment in a very real sense, and these choices are left embossed in physical form on our material selves."[3]

As the saying goes, "Wherever you go, there you are." There's no way that you can bring a new universe to life around you without changing who you are. You can't drag the same old you into your dream world. You won't go. You'll always want to keep one foot back in the familiar universe of yesterday. You can straddle two universes for only a short time before you must choose. Unfortunately, most people choose to return to the universe they know rather than persist in creating the one they want. They convince themselves that they don't deserve it, or that it's not possible, or that it's just too uncomfortable and weird.

This means that the first and most important step in launching your creative process is making a leap of faith. A leap so big that it actually propels you into another orbit in your life. You must choose to believe that this creative power belongs to you, that it is, in fact, your birthright, and that you are destined to master it.

You can take comfort in this fact: you are already exercising your possibility amplification powers. Look around you. You have created the world you live in now. The people you have drawn to you, the quality of the relationships you have, your career trajectory, how you feel about yourself and your situation every day, how connected you feel to the universe. These are your creations.

Perhaps you have not considered how much energy you are using to maintain the current state of affairs. I like to view my participation in the Possibility Amplification Process simply as an energy exchange, in which I take energy that I am currently spending to feel down, trapped, frustrated, unhappy, or stuck and repurpose it to feel engaged, motivated, content, and successful.

It takes some practice to develop this skill. I hung myself up for a long time thinking that I could not have it all. I didn't think I could do what I loved and also make a good living at it. I was afraid. Afraid of making a bad choice, of having to ask for help, of looking like an idiot who'd left a good paying job with great benefits. I had a million reasons for not doing with my very short life what I wanted to do, not the least of which was keeping a roof over my son's head. And for some reason, despite the fact that I was still alive, and no previous choice I'd ever made had killed me, and despite the fact that I was paying my bills handily and creating enormous career success, I somehow believed that I would not be able to figure this out. I'd even run my own business for eight years! So why did I not believe in myself?

And then I hit upon a truth: *it was because I wasn't spending any time believing in myself.* I certainly wasn't celebrating my splendor. Instead, I spent an enormous amount of time berating myself for my faults and mistakes, my social blunders and weaknesses. In retrospect, I can tell you it was an enormous waste of time. But more important, it constituted an enormous part of my day-to-day experience of life. I was, in fact, *creating* a life in which I wasn't very happy. I remember thinking at one point that my brain was completely in charge of me, and that it was so programmed with crap that I would never be able to get free. Luckily, that computer programming degree I'd gotten many years earlier came in handy. In time, I realized that I could reprogram my brain once I understood how. I finally integrated a message I'd heard or read in various forms many times over from other teachers: You have to assume control. You have to take a quantum leap of faith. You have to believe, whether it makes sense or not. Choose it, even if other people think you're crazy. They are not living your life. You are. You are the only one who can protect the integrity of your dreams. Don't give them up. Invest in them!

In my interview with Dr. Bruce Lipton, he cautioned me

about giving away my power or letting it be taken away. "If people show exceptional behaviors, they're shuttled off," he said. "In New Zealand, they have a saying for that: 'cutting the tall poppies.'" Once you begin to truly believe in your dream and your amplification process accelerates, you will meet with resistance. You will be asked to spend your energy on projects and people that will take you in the direction opposite of where you want to go. Meet resistance with resistance. Remember, there is still only a certain amount of energy in your system. Think of your energy as the most precious commodity you have, and make conscious choices about where you will spend it.

GIVE YOURSELF A BELIEF BATH: TOYS TO TAKE IN WITH YOU

Okay, let's go swimming! We want to drench ourselves in the belief that our vision is coming true. Like a raft floating in a pool, your belief can buoy you up. Like a rubber ducky, it can make you lighten up and laugh. Like playing with toy boats, practicing your belief can take your mind off your worries and help you refocus on your amplification process. Like a good bubble bath, your belief can calm you and reconnect you to your purpose. So jump in and let me show you my toys.

MEDITATION. It can change your brain. The Tibetan Dalai Lama has participated in brain research since the 1990s, dispatching some of his most experienced practitioners to the United States for testing. Researchers discovered that the monks' brains behave differently than the brains of those who do not meditate. Gamma waves moving through the monks' brains were more powerful, as were waves associated with perception, problem solving, and consciousness. The longer a monk had been practicing, the more pronounced the change in his brain.

But let's be real. You're not going to put ten thousand hours of meditation on your list of things to do, are you? Luckily this level of commitment is not a necessary component of the Possibility Amplification Process. But it might not be a bad idea to spend some time training your brain to generate the emotions you want to feel, to focus on the images you want to create, and to let go of the thoughts that do not serve you. Even a little dose of meditation might be able to help.

A PRACTICE OF CONTEMPLATION AND REFLECTION. If the word *meditation* brings up unpleasant images of twisting your legs into a pretzel and sitting with your backbone ramrod straight for thirty minutes while trying to think about nothing, then may I suggest this alternative? Spend regular time sitting with your thoughts about your amplification process. Go ahead and have that cup of coffee next to you. Maybe make this practice the first thing you do in the morning. Bring something to write with if you want. Sit in a comfy chair. Your examination and reinforcement of your beliefs doesn't have to be painful. It can be a fun mental journey through your wishes and dreams.

VISUALIZATION. We talked about visualization quite a bit in chapter 1. This is where you decide when you will do it. Right before you go to sleep at night? First thing in the morning, before the rest of the family is up? Creating a list of the things you want to visualize and assigning each thing to a day of the week might be one way to organize it. For example, you can picture yourself captaining your brand-new seventy-two-foot yacht on Monday, on Tuesday you can visualize your conversation with Oprah, on Wednesday you can envision yourself giving that award-acceptance speech you've been working on, and so on. What specific milestone events are part of your dream life? Can you see each one?

IMMERSIVE PROBLEM SOLVING. Do you believe it? Do it! Want to be the top salesperson in your company? Make those cold calls. Need to get folks to sponsor your bike trip across Italy? Set up that website. Want to buy a house on the water? Pick up real estate magazines and start visiting open houses. Nothing convinces your brain more than when you become actively involved according to your beliefs.

THE IMAGINED AUDIENCE. Tell the story of your success to an imaginary audience. By putting your passion into your words, you'll find yourself becoming more and more clear about what you want to create. It will begin to feel as if it is already a fait accompli. Imagine that you've been asked to give the commencement speech at a university. What will you tell your audience about what you've created in life? What keys to success will you pass on? You might also pretend to have a conversation with an old friend you haven't seen in a while, and imagine her amazement at how you've changed your life. Your confident report on the future will make you feel more confident about your amplification process in the present.

BLOGGING. The word *blog* is a shortened version of the term *web log*. You can share the process of amplifying your dream into reality by posting your progress online. Your collected posts will become a public journal of your success. Since others will see your posts, they may comment on them, and soon you may find yourself in a dialog with other like-minded people engaged in a similar process. Who knows? Your blog might end up being a bestselling book.

VLOGGING. This is much like blogging, only instead of typing you use a video camera to record each post. The cool thing about vlogging is that you will capture moments when you are deep in your belief about your Possibility Amplification Process, and other moments when you are not. Study the differences between the two. What inspired you to get so psyched up on one day and not on another? Did something specific happen? Did you wake up with excited, supportive thoughts in your head, for example? How do you look, sound, and act when you are totally on your own program? Does your language change? Practice being the inspired person you see in your posts.

JOURNALING. Write down your observations about your beliefs and about how your beliefs influence your behavior. Journaling, like many of the other toys here, is about creating awareness and recording the discoveries you make while being aware. Write down the reasons why you are destined to create your dream. Alternatively, write down the reasons why you will *not* successfully amplify your vision, and present a counterargument against each one. If you're distracted, a journal is a great place to dump all the thoughts spinning you around, so that you get them out of your head and on paper, and get back on track toward your dream.

PRAYER. Prayer comes in many forms, but it's basically communicating with the deity or higher power of your choice, according to the religious or spiritual tradition of your choice, to make requests regarding the creation of your dream life and to extend gratitude. Your prayer might be an expression of intention or belief, as well. As Jesus said, "All things are possible to him who believes."

PRE-THANKING. Lastly, you can thank the Powers That Be in advance, as if your dream creation has already come true. Pre-thanking is a great way to remind yourself of how you will feel once your vision has become reality, because it forces you to be mentally in the place where it's already happened.

By managing and nurturing your beliefs, you will create the right kind of internal environment, one that will keep you in growth mode and maximize the use of your energy. The second environment you need to be aware of is the one outside your body. The great news is that it's already aware of you.

4. DECOHERENCE

Living on the Edge between Possibility and Reality

REMEMBER WHEN I SAID you are the best-designed possibility amplifier in the universe? Well, I lied. You are the second-best-designed possibility amplifier in the universe. But that's okay, because you're partners with the possibility amplifier that's in first place. This partnership is productive, whether you've been aware of it or not. In just a bit, I'll reveal your secret connection, but first, let me share some background information.

For a couple of centuries, physicists have been trying to figure out how all the weirdness at the subatomic or quantum level of the universe ends up looking like the everyday world we see all around us. If you were a being at the subatomic level, you would have amazing superpowers. You could easily walk through walls, transport yourself to Cancún for a cocktail and back, be at work and home in bed at the same time, and send important information instantaneously to your boss, your spouse, or anyone else you were involved with, without a phone, a fax machine, a computer, or any other kind of communications device, no matter where in the universe they were. Wouldn't that be great? So, if everything — including us — is made up of quantum material, how come we can't do all that?

For a long time, scientists have thought all those wacky quantum possibilities simply cancel each other out. Those teeny events, when added up together and averaged, just happen to look like the world we expect and live in. Scientists call it "wave function collapse" but haven't been able to explain how it works or why it happens.

In 1952, David Bohm invented the theory of decoherence to explain why all the possibilities available at the quantum level of the universe do not appear in the world around us. Decoherence also served very well as a mechanical explanation for how wave function collapse happens. For about thirty years, with some exceptions, the theory was largely ignored. Then suddenly in the 1980s it became popular again, and now it's one of the hot topics of quantum physics, primarily because decoherence has been observed and proven in the lab. And that's great news for us, because decoherence happens to be one of the most powerful tools in the possibility amplifier's tool kit. It is *the* process by which quantum possibility becomes reality.

A quantum system can be defined as a group of independent but interrelated elements that behave according to the laws of quantum physics. The environment is everything else. Up until the recent past, quantum physicists always studied quantum systems in isolation. As silly as it might sound, no one was really taking the quantum environment into account, mathematically or otherwise. Once we turned our attention to it, it became clear that the environment has an incredibly powerful effect on quantum activity.

When a quantum system interacts with its environment, it's changed in a profound way. Before interacting with its environment, the system is in all possible states at once. That is, all the possibilities are available, as we discussed in chapter 1. Once the system and the environment start to interact, a preferred set of states is selected out of all the states the system has to offer. (This process is called *superselection*.) The rest of the information in the system — the other possibilities (or states) — is lost. To be more specific, all the other possibilities are still there, they're just not the ones that we see manifested in our three-dimensional reality. They're somewhere, just not here. And since we can no longer access them, we can ignore them. (For now. We'll come back to them later.)

If you were the environment, the quantum system would be like a magician asking you to the stage as a volunteer to pick a couple of cards from a deck fanned out in her hand. All of the possibilities are available to you. You can pick any card in the deck. And yet, as your hand passes over the fanned-out deck of cards, it's as if you feel hot spots — places in the deck you are drawn to and want to pick from. After you pick your cards, the rest of the cards magically disappear. Without looking at them, the magician guesses the cards you hold and asks you to hold them up and show them to the audience, which you do — and that's all anybody ever sees. Does the magician still have the other cards? Probably. Do we know where they are or how to find them? Not at the moment. But quantum physicists and their fans have a fantasy that one night, maybe even ten, twenty, or thirty years from now, they'll wait outside the stage door, wrestle the magician to the ground, and find the cards in some hidden pocket. Right now, we just don't know the trick.

So the question is, how did you, as the environment and stage volunteer, decide which cards were the right ones to choose and show to the audience? That is, how does the environment know which is the correct set of states, out of all the possible states inherent in a quantum system, to preserve and amplify into reality?

The first thing you did was look at the deck of cards — and that's what the environment is doing with *its* deck of cards. The environment is *monitoring* quantum activity.

I'm gonna give you a moment with that thought. It's powerful. What quantum physicists are saying today about decoherence is that the environment is an active observer. The implications of this proposal are vast. Not only are *we* watching, but . . . so is everything else. You know from chapter 1 that you can influence events in both the macro and the micro worlds just by observing them. Wouldn't it be potent to have the biggest observer in the universe help you *decohere* your vision? Later in this chapter, I'll provide you with some concrete ways to leverage the environment in your amplification process.

The second thing you did when making your card selections was to apply a sorting process to determine which cards to draw from the deck. When you're choosing random cards from a deck, isn't it almost as if you want the right cards to call to you? Isn't it as if, when your hand passes over them, they make your fingers tingle? We want to feel as if we are choosing the special cards, the magical ones. Again, the environment is doing the same thing. The states selected for amplification are the most powerful, robust, and stable ones, the ones with the most intense energy signatures.

A state is considered robust and stable if there is redundant information stored about it in the environment. For example, when we "see" a table, we actually see the many photons that it emits. Information about the table is recorded in each of the emitted photons. The dust motes that come into contact with the table also have a record of the table. The information embedded in the sound waves from someone dropping a book on the table is a record. The environment, which includes these photons, dust motes, sound waves, and other such recording entities, operates as a communications device to tell us what's there. What that means to us is, if we have a preferred state — or outcome — that we want to create out of all the energy we have available around us to manipulate and mold, we must create redundant information about it in our environment to make it robust.

So how do you do that? Let's say you want to own a particular car. That is the preferred outcome you would like to bring to life in this reality. A quantum system describing it would perhaps offer the following possibilities: You can have any car. You can have no car. You can have a motorcycle. You can have a bike. You can have the car of your dreams. The *preferred* choice is the one that seems to be strongest. To make your preferred outcome stronger, begin creating and pouring redundant information about your ownership of this car into the environment.

There's a bunch of particularly effective ways to create redundant information about this outcome. You could visit a dealership, for example, and get prices. You could take the car for a test drive. Then later, when you visualize yourself owning and driving this car — visualization being another way to create redundant information about this outcome — you'll know what it feels like to drive the car. You can hang pictures of the car at home and at work, where you'll be sure to see them frequently. You can hum the manufacturer's jingle to yourself. If it's a really good jingle, you can sing it to your friends. You can check into financing. If you need to save money for the down payment, you can open a savings account and start putting money in it. You can choose paint and interior colors. You can tell your friends that you will soon own that car. You can write a journal entry about how excited you are that you own this car. You can clean out the garage for it. If there's a car giveaway contest with your car as a prize, you can enter the contest. You can find an online users group of people who own that car and start a conversation with them. Heck, you can even shave the car's logo into your dog's fur. The more you imprint the environment with information about your desired outcome, the more likely it is that the environment will support it.

It's important to note, then, that it is the *system* that influences the *environment*, not the other way around, because the nature of the system determines which states are most robust and stable. The environment just supports the amplification of those robust and stable states. So, if you're a system coming to the creation party, you are the guest of honor. You're the one who gets to pick what will be created.

In chapter 1, I pointed out how, by observing a single photon pass through the slits in the double slit experiment, we created an inescapable history for that particle that it had to obey. The redundant-information aspect of decoherence is another method for creating a history to "back up" your desired future state. Quantum physics says that in order for a possibility's history to be consistent enough to support its amplification, the records of its existence in the environment must be found by different observers.

When you go talk to the financing guy at the car dealership, and you take the test-drive with the sales guy, these observers become witness to your dream. To these witnesses, the fact that you are going to buy this car is a probability, not a dream. In that way, as objective observers of each other's dreams, maybe we're *all* in the dream business. Doesn't it make you want to support the dreams of others when you know you are part of their observing environment?

Kiplinger's Personal Finance magazine reported on one such dreamer, David Lent. David wanted to film a documentary about why some people are successful. He got this idea in 1987 while reading a magazine article. Since he already had a thriving business with his wife, Susan, he began to interview people on the side about how they'd made it. By 1999, it became clear that it would take more money than he had to get the celebrity interviews he needed to sell the documentary. But it wasn't until 2004 that he decided to try the "visualize your outcome" technique. He imagined that a company called Wellspring Media, the perfect distributor for his project, had purchased it and was marketing it. He copied the company's logo on a card, wrote "This is my distributor" on it, and put it on his desk. He called Wellspring. He emailed Wellspring. He got no response. He knew that Wellspring had representatives who sold to video stores, so he went to a local video store and asked them for the name of their sales representative. This is where the magic starts: the sales rep knew Wellspring's former CEO and got the two of them together. The CEO invested fifty thousand dollars in the project. David finished the project, Wellspring became his distributor, and PBS picked up the series. *David had successfully decohered his dream into reality.* Last we heard from David, he was buying an Airstream touring coach to head off on his promotional tour.

Imagine what might have happened if David had started his decoherence program back in 1987, when he first read that article. His dream could have come true a lot sooner.

You, too, have complete control over the creation of redundant information about your desired outcome, so that's a blessing. But you don't have control over everything in your environment, and neither does a quantum system. In the interaction between a quantum system and its environment, some of the system's possible states will get quantumly entangled with parts of the environment. This is bad news for those particular states, because that entanglement spells their certain doom. Entangled states are not considered strong enough to be selected for amplification, so you won't be seeing them in this world anytime soon.

Entanglement can tie *you* up as a possibility amplifier, too. Let's say one of your very good friends tells you that you'll never be able to afford that car of your dreams. This puts before you a set of optional responses. First of all, you might want to reconsider your friendship. Second, if you get entangled with that part of your environment and decide to dance with that person mentally — maybe by saying to yourself: "Yeah, she's right, I know; I can't afford this car, I'll never have this car" — you've just shifted some power away from your desired state of owning the car. If you really want the car, you can't allow that to happen. Refuse to become entangled with parts of your environment that don't support the creation of your desired outcome. Hold really tightly to your vision, no matter the circumstances. You have to throw off entanglements that will suppress the outcome you want and support the creation of a state you don't want. Unfortunately, there's plenty of entanglement to avoid, because there are so many possibilities. One friend might say you can't afford that car. Another might say, "How about a Volkswagen instead?" Another might say, "You can always take the bus!" And I'll just get in trouble if I talk about what your mother might say.

Here's an example of what I mean. Recently I went through a period of about a year in which I suffered repetitive bladder and kidney infections. I ended up in the hospital twice. The first urologist I went to said that I had interstitial cystitis, which is chronic irritation of the lining of the bladder wall. He told me that this means there are little fissures or cracks in the lining of the bladder wall that will never go away. Eating or drinking the wrong things would irritate them, so I'd have this irritated feeling all the time. And, because of the fissures, bacteria would find it easier to hang on to the bladder's lining, so I'd keep getting these infections.

Right away I decided that I wasn't going to have a chronic health problem like that, so I decided I didn't have interstitial cystitis. The doctor proceeded to treat me as if I had it anyway, and gave me a list of about four hundred foods I should eliminate from my diet, along with a prescription for prophylactic antibiotics, which I should take for three days starting as soon as I felt the symptoms.

Well, I'd been on antibiotics nonstop, it seemed to me, for almost a year, and the last thing I wanted was more antibiotics. They were making me sicker than the sickness! The last straw was when I discovered that one of the antibiotics I was taking was probably causing the tendonitis problem I was having in my Achilles tendon (right) and my thigh (left). Since I'm a runner, and for months hadn't really been able to run, this helped motivate me to get off the antibiotics for good.

After some months, the first doctor told me to go get a very expensive scan of my urinary tract to make sure there weren't any anatomical problems. At this point I realized I was being treated as if I had a particular condition for which apparently I had not even been appropriately diagnosed. That's when I got a new urologist. On my first visit, I demanded an accurate diagnosis. On my second visit, I had a cystoscopy, which is a look inside the bladder, and guess what? I didn't have interstitial cystitis! I could have just accepted the first doctor's recommendations, gotten entangled with his diagnosis, believed it, taken four hundred foods out of my diet, and started living as if I had a chronic condition that I did not have. But I chose not to get entangled with that doctor and instead stayed firm in my belief that I didn't have cystitis, and I don't.

And after that, it became clear that I couldn't have any more infections, because eventually these infections would damage my organs. One day I was driving in the car with the love of my life, Michael, and in his concern for me, he implied that he believed I was going to continue having infections. I said, "No, I'm not! Stop sending me that negative energy! I'm sticking to my belief. I'm not going to continue having infections, I'm not taking any more antibiotics, a year is long enough, I don't have interstitial cystitis — I'm done!" I refused to get entangled with his then-current (and somewhat flawed) belief system. Fortunately, Michael is very astute, and he agreed directly that I was healed. That turned out to be a wise decision, because after a couple more sporadic bouts, I haven't had a single problem.

Refusing to get entangled with your environment is one way to ensure that the outcome you want is the one that gets selected because it is the most robust. Belief is enormously important, as we saw in chapter 3 — combine it with holding tight to your vision. Don't let *anybody* tell you that you can't!

I had a moment of weakness on my health issue when my mother told me that it sounded like interstitial cystitis. That really got me, because my mother is a fabulous diagnostician. Although not a doctor, she's a medical professional, and she's a better diagnostician than most doctors I know. One day she said, "You probably have it." And I said, "I'm not *having* that, Mom. Don't say it!" She said, "Okay. But a lot of women do have it." And I countered with: "I'm not a lot of women! I'm not having this," to which she said, "Okay." And then right before I went in for the cystoscopy, she called me to say, "I don't think you have interstitial cystitis. Because your symptoms don't match up." And I said, "I *know*. Of *course* I don't have interstitial cystitis." She finally came around and got entangled with *me* and with the robust state I was trying to create. My mom's always trying to support me. That's one of the many reasons why I love her.

What's really cool about the environment and how it can work *with* you to create the outcome you want is that according to decoherence, the environment is all about suppressing interference between the outcomes you don't want — what I call the anti-outcomes — and the outcomes you do want. It's important to know that suppression can happen very quickly, so if you have been applying a decoherence strategy to the creation of your vision, be forewarned. One of your desired outcomes might happen way before you expect it to. Will you really be ready?

You might think that's a silly question. "Yeah, I'm ready to receive a million dollars right now," you might be saying to yourself. But are you really? What bank do you want to put that money in? What kind of account would be the best to hold it? Have you planned how to invest that money? What kind of return do you want to get? Will you live on that return, spend part of the million, or spend the whole thing? What will you do when your friends, family, and strangers start asking you for money? There's almost a question for every dollar! And this applies to that giant order for your products you've been envisioning, getting all those new clients you've been needing, or finding the love of your life.

If you think you're ready right this second for the life of your dreams, then here are some tips for accelerating decoherence.

BREAKING THE PRESENT
TO MAKE ROOM FOR THE FUTURE:
THE FIVE TOP DECOHERENCE TECHNIQUES

Tip #1. Don't Measure the Environment

What's very funny — well, to me, but I've been reading this stuff for a long time — is that quantum physicists are getting paid big bucks to figure out how to *stifle* decoherence, in order to create quantum computers that really work. It seems that because decoherence and contact with the environment take the "quantum" out of "quantum computing," there's a whole new field devoted to quashing decoherence, a phenomenon that happens everywhere, all the time. Needless to say, this is a tall order. Here's the first sentence of a summary of an article published in *Physical Review A*: "We analyze and compare three different strategies, all aimed at controlling and eventually halting decoherence."[1] Yikes! That's not our goal at all. Fortunately, you're not trying to build a successful quantum computer; you're creating the life of your dreams. The strategies outlined in that article are your *anti*strategies.

Here's one of those antistrategies: take a measurement of the environment. By doing so, some physicists argue, you can effectively invert decoherence in many cases, blocking the interaction between the environment and the system. Here's how it works: As a system comes in contact with the environment, and the environment begins to amplify the most robust states available in that system, bits of classical information "leak" into the environment from the system. (In other words, the most robust possibilities begin to come true.) If you choose to erase, ignore, or otherwise disenfranchise the bits of your dream as they begin to manifest, you can completely reverse the progress you've made so far.

To illustrate, let's stick to our car metaphor. If you've posted pictures of your dream car all over your house, and one day in a fit of impatience you rip them all down and throw them away, you've begun the inversion of the decoherence process. If you went to talk to the dealership about financing, and then they call you up to confirm the low interest rate they quoted and ask when you can come in, you can chuck the whole thing by saying, "Even at that rate, I can't really afford the car," and hang up.

However, the most painful inversion of decoherence I've ever seen is the one in which we paint a mental picture of how we think the environment is viewing *us* — including our friends, our family, our coworkers, and so on — and then, as a result of our discomfort with that vision, we abandon our dreams in full retreat. We pull back every bold thing we've done, every record of our dream's temporary existence, and give up. The false measurement on which we've based these actions kills both our dream and our belief in our ability to create it.

Recall that the way we measure things is extraordinarily

powerful. Look to the end of this chapter for another amazing secret about measurement.

Tip #2. The Three R's: Repetition, Repetition, Repetition

Remember, stability is a critical factor in the environment's selection of states to amplify. The environment wants to know that you'll keep it up! Quantum physicists check on this quality by reading the trajectory of a system or part of a system over time to see if it's on track. What trajectories are you painting on the backdrop of the universe?

If the trajectory you're painting is: "My boss says I have one more chance before I get suspended," and you are counting on the suspension as the safeguard between you and no job, you're painting the wrong trajectory. That may seem obvious to you. A less obvious example might be: "I've been doing some things to make my dream come true, but then I quit for a while, because I just kind of ran out of belief." Letting the trajectory of your success peter out creates an unstable waveform that the universe will find too weak to support.

The cool thing about action and belief is that each feeds off the other. If you're not feeling a strong belief about the validity of your dream, take some action to revitalize your belief. If you're feeling a strong belief in your dream, taking action turns your belief into tangible results. To demonstrate your willingness to maintain belief in and support of your dream state, take repetitive action toward your dream.

Tip #3. Heat It Up

Decoherence happens faster over time, as long as the interaction with the environment is consistent. So be persistent with the actions that lead to your dreams, but also do them frequently to create change quickly.

I had an analogy about this that involved imagining yourself as a prizefighter in the ring. You throw a punch, and it lands soundly on your opponent's head. Good for you! You throw the next punch . . . three months later. This will not likely win you the fight. Your opponent will be very busy in between punches, and the match will be over before it even began.

After I came up with that analogy, I decided I didn't like it, because decoherence is not about fighting the environment; it's about cooperating with the environment and taking what the environment has to offer. So I decided it's more like eating an ice cream cone on a hot summer day. If you want to eat the ice cream, you have to lick it. And if you want to eat *all* the ice cream, rather than have it run down your arm, you'd better lick fast! This advice applies to other areas of life as well, but that's a different book.

Or maybe not. There's an interesting property of the universe called entropy, which means that the universe is always trying to achieve equilibrium, or even things out. So when your dream system and the environment come into contact, they do a little dance called entropy exchange in order to accomplish that. Entropy exchange in decoherence is written in the physics literature as S_{EX}. So there you have it: confirmation that creating your dreams is S_{EX}y. But I probably didn't have to tell *you* that.

Tip #4. Opposites Attract

To speed up decoherence, choose and perform actions that differ significantly from the ones you would normally choose and perform. By doing so, you can strengthen yourself against entanglement. When you stretch yourself, you send a message to the environment saying that your dream is the most robust state available. If you want to *really* stretch, look to your fears to come up with ideas of what these actions might be. For example, if you're afraid of public speaking, go speak in public about some aspect of your dream. If your dream is to meet the love of your life, and you normally wouldn't walk up to someone at a bar, try it out.

Tip #5. Dream a Little Dream

In this chapter, I described David Lent and how visualization caused his dream to decohere into this reality, including the appearance of money, contacts, interviews, a distributorship, and a buyer. Visualization is an enormously powerful tool, and in decoherence it helps create the robust states that the environment chooses to help you amplify into reality.

In the last year of a corporate job I'd held for eight years, I wrote myself a note and filed it away in my goal book: "I hereby predict that I will be separated from my company with a severance package of one year's salary, and that will be just fine with me." One year later, it came true, and I used that seed money to finance the start-up of my current business.

What's on your visualization roster? Choose something you've decided to create in your life, and spend five or ten minutes visualizing that outcome today. Make a written record of what you visualize. Your records of your creation will begin to have an impact on your environment.

So besides the fact that the environment is monitoring quantum activity, some physicists would say that the environment is taking measurements. And if it's taking *measurements*, then it's applying the Zeno effect, which I talk about in the next chapter. Measurements in quantum activity are incredibly powerful, and they are actually powerful in our everyday world, if you know what and how to measure. The "how" is the most important part. By measuring properly, you can have an enormous impact on your progress. And that's certainly true at the quantum level of the universe. In fact, it just might be that decoherence and the Zeno effect are opposite sides of the same coin.

5. THE INVERSE ZENO EFFECT

Accelerating the Realization of Your Dreams

WHAT IF YOU COULD STOP THE WORLD FROM SPINNING just by repeatedly measuring how fast it turned? Or stop a wineglass from falling off the counter by repeatedly measuring how far it had fallen? Better yet, what if you could cut your time on the treadmill by measuring how many miles you'd already run? Or finish projects in record time by measuring how close you were to completion? What if, just by measuring, you could slow things down, stop them, or speed them up?

Quantum physicists are already controlling the activity of subatomic particles just by measuring it. W. M. Itano, D. J. Heinzen, J. J. Bollinger, and D. J. Wineland of the National Institute of Standards and Technology in Boulder, Colorado, the first to conduct an experiment in which they did just that, published their results in 1990.[1]

Although much earlier work by Leonid Khalfin of the former USSR and others paved the way, this phenomenon was formulized and named in 1977 by B. Misra and E. C. G. Sudarshan of the Center for Particle Theory at the University of Texas at Austin.[2]

They dubbed it the quantum Zeno effect, with a tip of the hat to the Greek philosopher Zeno of Elea. Zeno was the author of a collection of paradoxes — a paradox being a statement that appears to be true but which logically contradicts itself — that he used to support the philosophical arguments of his teacher, Parmenides. The purpose of both Parmenides's teachings and Zeno's paradoxes was to challenge the everyday perception of the real world, much like quantum reality challenges our historical view of how the universe works.

One of Zeno's paradoxes, known as the Arrow, inspired the name of the quantum effect I am about to describe. In it, Zeno argued that motion is an illusion. When an arrow is in flight, he said, at any given instant the arrow is only in one place and, therefore, at rest. Adding up all these "rests" cannot equal motion, any more than adding many zeros together will give you a sum greater than zero. As a result, the arrow cannot be said to be "moving," since it is always at rest. See the strange dilemma?

Similarly, thought Misra and Sudarshan, if you repeatedly measure a quantum system that's in the process of evolving — that is, changing between one state and another — it would never be able to evolve, because each measurement would require the system to remain in the state being measured. In other words, the system can't be in motion, because we're always observing it "at rest." They even originally referred to this effect as the quantum Zeno *paradox*.

If you think of "measurement" as a special form of observation, this conclusion makes sense. As you may remember from chapter 1, our observation modifies outcome at the subatomic level of the universe. A measurement requires that we observe the state of the quantum system. If we can observe it multiple times at very short intervals — and by short, I mean microseconds apart — the quantum system is forced to choose and offer one possible state to be measured, rather than remain in a state of superposition.

In the 1990 experiment by Itano and his colleagues (known as the "IHBW experiment," an abbreviation of the authors' names), this measurement effect was physically observed. Beryllium ions were confined in a device called an ion trap. A radio frequency field was applied to force the ions from a low energy state to a higher energy state. Very brief pulses of light were used to measure the state of the ions at regular intervals.

When no measurements were taken during a certain period of time, all the ions were found in the higher energy state. When measurements were taken during a comparable period of time, this was no longer true. Rather, some ions were in the higher energy state, and some in the lower. As the number of measurements increased, the ions were more likely to be in the lower energy state, right where they started. It was as if the experimenters were repeatedly asking the ions, "Are you still in the lower energy state?" and the more often they asked the question, the more likely the answer was yes. By their measurement alone, the scientists were able to control quantum events and slow them down. They pulled the ions back to their starting point just by asking if they were still there.

It's also possible to speed up quantum events via measurement, which is known as the inverse Zeno effect. An experiment carried out by M. C. Fischer, B. Gutiérrez-Medina, and M. G. Raizen of the University of Texas at Austin in 2001 was the first observation of both the Zeno effect and the inverse Zeno effect in a single experiment.[3] A system was created in which sodium atoms were held captive in a wave of light. Over time and under certain conditions, all the sodium atoms eventually escaped the wave of light by tunneling. Tunneling is the capability of subatomic particles to cross seemingly impenetrable barriers, and it's a very common phenomenon at the subatomic level of the universe.

Through regular and periodic measurements of the system, Fischer and his colleagues were able to both slow down (Zeno effect) and speed up (inverse Zeno effect) the evolution of the system. They discovered that the sodium atoms were able to escape at a much higher rate when the measurements taken were spaced more widely apart. How come?

Giving the quantum system more time between measurements to evolve farther from its initial state resulted in changing the essential nature of the measure. Rather than asking, "Are you still trapped in there?" the scientists were in effect asking the sodium particles: "Have you escaped yet?" By getting out in front of the process, they actually created a path that drew the process along that path in an accelerated way. In other words, just the act of taking measurements applied the inverse Zeno effect and caused more sodium particles to escape.

So while a colloquialism that expresses the Zeno effect is that "a watched pot never boils," the inverse Zeno effect could be expressed as: "You can boil the pot by watching." Or more specifically, by measuring.

THE POWER OF MEASUREMENT

In our everyday lives too, measurement causes amazing things to happen, many of which we take for granted. By measuring the ingredients you use while cooking, you end up with things like delicious desserts and meals, whereas not measuring can result in gelatinous goop or dried-up food Frisbees. By repeatedly measuring the balance in your checking account, you're more likely to have money in it at the end of the month, instead of being overdrawn. By regularly measuring the amount of fuel left in your car's tank, you happily fill up when you're supposed to and motor along, rather than getting stuck on the side of the road. Every day you're taking millions of measurements, and you're probably not even aware of it.

In business, measuring alone drives significant results. A 2000 survey of its own executives conducted by the United Way revealed that implementing program outcome measurement resulted in better communication of results to stakeholders, more staff focus on common goals, and more successful competition for resources and funding. So, they were able to tell their story better, which brought in more funding. They created more cultural alignment in their local offices. They more effectively used their resources, which enabled them to provide better service to their communities. This wasn't a strategic overhaul, by any means. The only thing that changed was that measures were established, tracked, and reported.

In *Good to Great*, Jim Collins cites the example of a biotechnology company called Amgen, cofounded by George Rathmann in 1980. In twenty years, Amgen grew from a start-up to a consistently profitable company worth $3.2 billion. When asked how he did it, Rathmann referred back to his experiences where he had worked previously, at Abbott Laboratories: "What I got from Abbott was the idea that when you set your objectives for the year, you record them in concrete. You can change your plans throughout the year, but you never change what you measure yourself against." Rathmann learned the discipline of sticking to a measure, and he established that same culture at Amgen with amazing results.[1]

According to an article in the journal *Purchasing*, the U.S.-based Stratex Networks, a manufacturer of wireless and network management products, used measurement as the common language it shared with Taiwan-based Microelectronics Technology, to which it outsourced a major part of its manufacturing in 2002.

The two companies needed a way to keep their efforts synchronized in order to keep customers happy and costs down. A new set of measurements was established to manage this critical overseas relationship between the two companies, which spans time zones and cultures. "The metrics have helped to address these challenges," said Robert Schlaefi, vice president of global operations for Stratex. Not only had product quality improved because of the shared responsibility for achieving the metrics, he said, but Stratex had "also seen a substantial reduction in our manufacturing costs. In fact, we were able to cut these costs in half."[5]

By instituting a measuring system alone, these companies created fantastic results. Key metrics — that is, the selected few measurements that drive core results and bring a personal or business vision to fruition — can actually get you where you want to go, and faster too. We'll talk more about how to determine if a measurement is a key metric later in this chapter.

My husband, Michael, runs a technology company. During a staff meeting, Michael raised an issue that had been bothering him for some time: the frequency of visits by individual users to the company's many websites. It was a metric always listed on the reports, but was seldom discussed, and the number hadn't changed for years. Michael said, "You know why that number hasn't changed? Because you're not measuring it." This met with some confusion from his staff. Of course we're measuring it, they said. It's right there on the report. "No. You're not," Michael insisted. "You're *recording* it. If you were measuring it, you'd be focused on it. You'd be looking for best practices. You'd set a goal for what you think it *should* be. You'd be thinking of ways to make that number change. But since you're *not* measuring it, nothing will happen."

Michael is very smart. He understands the power of measurement in driving business results: you get what you measure. You can apply the power of measurement to your personal performance in order to accelerate it and get the results you want. To do so, you'll need to learn to measure yourself the right way and at the right times.

THE POWER OF PERSONAL MEASUREMENT

First, let's take a look at how you typically measure yourself. Have you ever been in a situation where you said to yourself, "Geez! I can't believe I just *said* that!" Or: "I can't believe I *did* that! What was I *thinking*?" As human beings, we have a tendency to measure ourselves in the wrong places and at the wrong times — that is, at the negative moments. On top of that, we weigh our negative measures of ourselves more heavily than the positive. You're supposed to be humble, right? So when you're congratulated or talked up by someone else, you practice saying "thank you" with humility and gratitude, and you move the conversation on. In other words, you don't spend nearly as much time reveling in your successes as you do wallowing in your failures.

You also don't measure consistently. There are all kinds of reasons for that inconsistency, including your emotional state. If you feel good, you measure one way. If you feel down, you measure another. Some days you really pay attention to certain measurements, and other days you forget all about them. The main thrust is that you don't have a self-measurement system.

Wait! I take that back. You *do* have a self-measurement system. You just don't know what it is.

Every day, besides all the measurements you take of the outside world, such as checking your bank balance and your fuel gauge, you're taking thousands of measurements of yourself and how you're performing in the world. You notice if you're having a good hair day or bad, if you're being kind or bitchy, if you're being productive or distracted. Each of these measurements is based on — guess what? Your belief system. Your brain uses these thousands of daily measurements to back up your belief system. If your belief system says, "It's important for me to look good every day," then recording a bad hair day reinforces that belief (albeit negatively) and lets you know that today is not one of those days. If your belief system says, "I must demonstrate emotional control in front of others and keep a calm appearance," then catching yourself in a cranky moment — even one that's warranted — will tell you that you're in violation of your belief system, that you've fallen short of your expectations for yourself once again. After a day of many interruptions, you might say to yourself, "I got *nothing* done today!" when in fact you did many positive things that you haven't given yourself credit for. Are you getting the sense that measurements of this sort might do more harm than good?

If so, you're right. These are the kinds of measurements that produce the Zeno effect. By catching yourself repeatedly in violation of your own belief system, you constantly remind yourself of your own internal misalignment. As if you were walking in a pair of high heels with one heel broken, every step reminds you that something's wrong and the problem is you. By pitting yourself against yourself, you can slow down your progress until it doesn't feel like you're moving at all. After all, you're your own well-matched and formidable opponent. If you're looking for acceleration, this is not the way to go about it.

What about those positive measurements that you must be taking too? Well, let me ask you this: How many times did you smile to yourself today over something you did that was brilliant? I mean, even if nobody else noticed, you felt really good about having achieved something important to you, and you had a little personal celebration. Was it as many times as you clunked yourself on the brain for being an idiot, missing the mark, wasting time, or messing up? No? Really? Shocking.

Welcome to the human condition. Our personal measurement systems are twisted and biased; they're based on a convoluted collection of expectations we've absorbed over our lifetimes. If you are unfortunate enough to have others measuring you as well (and if you don't, I want to live where you live), you may be suffering from the effects of having multiple and possibly — or probably — conflicting measurement systems dictating how you feel about yourself every day and affecting your creative process. Luckily, there are clear-cut ways to leverage your personal measurement system in order to apply the inverse Zeno effect and speed you on your way.

TURNING ON THE INVERSE ZENO EFFECT: YOUR PERSONAL ROCKET LAUNCHER

The evolution of your vision can be sped up or slowed down by measuring it. Up until now, the focus of your personal measurement system has been, I'm willing to guess, judgment. Are you good or are you bad? Are you acceptable or unacceptable? Are you "appropriately" conforming or acting weird? The problem is that judgment-based measurement primarily produces one thing: judgment. Which doesn't really drive results.

By judging yourself, you can make yourself feel great, bad, or about the same as you do right now. While you're feeling great, you might be more productive. Or because you're happy with yourself, you might decide to take the afternoon off as a reward. No guarantees of improving results there. If you succeed in making yourself feel bad, you might bear down and try harder for a while and get more done. You might also experience depression, during which you'll find it hard to get anything done. If your judgment of yourself leaves you right where you are — "Yep, that's right, I did just as I expected" — is it a desirable place, or would you rather be somewhere else along the path in your personal development? Judgment raises many philosophical questions, but it's not the most valuable tool in creating the life of your dreams.

Dr. Joyce Ehrlinger, director of the Self and Social Judgment Lab at the Department of Psychology at Florida State University, has noted, "Those who possess great skill are uniquely aware not only of what they do know but also of what they do not yet know. This awareness can lead to underconfidence." In other words, even if we possess adequate skill to get the job done, we sell ourselves short by judging ourselves too harshly.[6]

The level of confidence you have in your ability to bring your vision to life will affect your ability to do so, and in tangible ways. One of the most likely ways, and one I bet you're familiar with, is procrastination. Dr. Piers Steel of the University of Calgary conducted an in-depth analysis of 691 research sources on the causes of procrastination. The number one cause? Lack of confidence.[7]

So judging yourself can cause underconfidence, and underconfidence causes procrastination. You keep putting things off, so nothing gets done. Nothing gets done, and you feel badly about yourself. Applying that judgment causes more procrastination. A vicious circle ensues in which you long for things but never get them, while all along you have exactly the skill set you need to bring your vision to life. Talk about measurement dysfunction!

As Dr. Steel says, "The old saying is true: whether you believe you can or believe you can't, you're probably right."[8] The old saying now has 691 studies to back it up. The great news is that measurement dysfunction can be fixed by conducting what I call a measurement intervention.

CONDUCTING YOUR
PERSONAL MEASUREMENT INTERVENTION

The first step in turning your personal measurement system into something that serves you rather than something you serve is to *change the reason why you measure*. Rather than using measurement as a gauge of your personal value, decide instead to measure yourself to gain important information that you can use to guide your creative process. The purpose of even having a measurement system is to create value. When it's your personal measurement system, it should create value for *you*. By changing the context of your measurement system from judgment to positive reinforcement of your creative process, you can reap more benefit from it.

Now, this doesn't mean you will instantly stop taking deleterious measurements of yourself, but it does mean you can decide how you will interpret those measurements. First, you can ask yourself if the measurement is true or false. If it shores up a belief that you've decided to remove from your belief system, then you can discard the measurement as well. For example, if you come up with the measurement "I got *nothing* done today!" it might shore up an outdated belief, such as "I will never achieve my vision because the world won't let me" or "I have absolutely no discipline." Of course, you have numerous possible responses. In the old context, you might feel badly. Perhaps frustrated. Angry. Disappointed in yourself.

In the new context of using measurements as information that will guide your creative process, you can choose a different response. You can make a list of all the things you did get done, negating your incorrectly perceived lack of discipline. You can remember that you gave your time to a friend or client because he needed you, and that being needed is, in fact, part of your vision. You can decide that the interruptions you tolerated today are not acceptable and block out time on your calendar during which you will be unavailable and will focus more intently on your creative efforts. When you use self-measurement to provide information, you have a wider array of possibilities to choose from that can eliminate the negative emotional drag on your creative process as well as spur you toward your goals.

It will be hard at first to divorce yourself from your addiction to self-judgment. You might feel like you're kidding yourself or that you're full of you-know-what. It's okay. Go ahead and have the battle with your brain. It's just following a well-entrenched script that you and your brain have practiced over and over together. It doesn't necessarily mean the script is right. It just means it's ingrained. Over time, the more often you remember that your self-measurement system is designed to serve *you*, the easier it will become to choose different responses.

Here's a tool you can use to turn a bad measurement into a good one: do a performance analysis. A performance analysis is basically the process of asking analytical questions to determine why a measurement is what it is. In the earlier example of feeling like you haven't gotten much done today, an undesirable measurement, you could ask questions like:

> Did I actually get something productive done today? (Yes.)
>
> Why do I feel I got nothing done? (The things I did were not related to my vision.)
>
> What was the first thing that got me off course? (I got stuck dealing with the email in my in-box.)
>
> How can I correct for that in the future? (Shut down my email software when I need to work on my vision.)
>
> Was there a moment during the day when I could have turned the day around? (Yes, when I glanced at my vision board while I was on the phone.)
>
> Is this a repetitive pattern or an isolated incident? (Repetitive.)
>
> If this is a repetitive pattern, what are my options for disrupting it? (Not launching my email software for the first hour that I'm at my desk, so I can plan my day.)

By implementing the findings of your performance analysis, you can tweak your creation process and make it more productive for you.

When you find yourself asking these questions naturally, you can be sure that you're applying the inverse Zeno effect. The more frequently you record the answers to these questions and refer back to them, the more you will learn about yourself and be able to take advantage of that knowledge to accelerate your creation process. When you prioritize knowledge over judgment, your modified measurement system becomes a powerful yet gentle guide.

When judgment has been removed from your measurement system, you'll find that reward and punishment disappear too. If you are neither "good" nor "bad," there's nothing to reward or punish. It's just you rocketing toward your dreams.

PICKING THE RIGHT MEASURES

What are you measuring about yourself right now? If you're a well-socialized individual, I can give you a hint: everything. The tribe known as human beings has a rule for just about every aspect of your behavior, looks, health, emotions, expression, and so on, and you are constantly comparing yourself to thousands of these acceptability measures daily. You likely also belong to subtribes, such as your family, which have their own sets of measures to meet. Unfortunately, most of these measures are not serving you. They're designed to serve the people around you.

Most of us are taught the importance of conforming to the Tribe, with a capital T, at an early age. The Tribe wants you to be a good member. It'll be happy for you if you make your dreams come true, but not necessarily if you break some of the Tribe's rules to get it done. The question is, how much of your energy will you spend on caring? Because if you're focused on meeting a wide range of tribal standards rather than on the few key standards that will drive the amplification of your vision, guess what wins?

Establishing a small collection of the right measures of your vision will create focus. Maybe even more important, it will *switch* your focus. Focus is another powerful form of our old friend, observation. By turning your mental and emotional energy to what you wish to create, less of that energy is available to focus on that which you do *not* wish to create. The Tribe may want you to value security over risk, or production over contentedness, or homemade cupcakes over a night out with friends, even if those things are in direct contradiction to your vision. Tending to and prioritizing the achievement of your vision's key measures will help you make decisions about the expenditure of your most valuable commodities: time and energy.

I belong to a women's business group called the Commonwealth Institute. A differentiating feature of this organization is that it offers membership in forum groups of eight to ten women that meet monthly to help each other achieve their goals. When this book was about half written, it was my turn to present the state of my business and ask for support. I presented a current list of my top four values. I informed the group that I had discarded some of my old measurements and created new ones. These new measurements were more focused on the outcomes I desired for my own creative process. Consequently, I told them, I would not be doing any marketing or prospecting in the fourth quarter. I would be finishing this book you hold in your hands. I would take only business that came to me.

How would this shift in focus change my behavior? As I explained to my colleagues, I had to stop doing marketing activities. This would be difficult for me, since I love marketing, I'm good at it, and it's easy for me to do. Marketing was a great distraction from sitting down and writing for extended periods of time.

I also had to manage my fear about not pursuing revenue. Having been self-employed for many years, I know that if you turn off the revenue machine for whatever reason, it takes a bit of cranking to turn it back on. I would have to value my vision more than my immediate financial security.

To make my new goals measurable, I would have to have deadlines. I announced that I would finish the book by the end of that year, along with a formal business plan. I would also send my book proposal to twenty-five agents by mid-November. (Can you see that I have a slight tendency to overcommit?)

During the meeting, and before I announced that I would not be pursuing new revenue generation in the fourth quarter, one of the women asked me if I intended to turn some new business activities into revenue producers. This was exactly the sort of question I expected to get from this particular tribe, which was established to create business success for its members. My fourth-quarter strategy was somewhat counterintuitive to the rules. Since I had just defined new key measures that supported the realization of my vision, I was able to resist the tribal pull, but that doesn't mean I didn't feel it. In my preparation the night before, I had had moments when I questioned my own sanity. I wondered if I would look naive in front of these seasoned business professionals, even though I'm a seasoned business professional myself. I wondered if being financially secure should come first. Ultimately, I decided that those things would not get me to my vision, whereas the measures I had defined would. I chose to invest in my vision and went forward with my presentation.

So, what happened right after the meeting? One of the women in the group called to hire me. Another friend and prospect sent me an email to rekindle our conversation about working together. A client referred two of her colleagues. Just like that, the cash flow concern evaporated. I found myself energized by the urgency of the work before me and the accountability I now had to the group, and began to devote large chunks of time to writing and research. Simply by choosing powerful measures that supported the amplification of my vision, I created a focus that set a whole collection of possibilities in motion that I could not have foreseen.

THE RIGHT WAY TO MEASURE

At the beginning of a measurement intervention, you redefine the context in which you measure yourself: you modify it to serve you in a positive way, rather than use it to judge, punish, or reward. Then you choose the right measures, the ones that will drive the realization of your vision. Lastly, you fine-tune the measures so that they will produce the most value.

A quality measurement is about outcomes, not outputs. An outcome is an end result or condition that you would like to create. In a business, a preferable outcome is profitability. In relationships, an outcome might be a happy marriage. In regard to your health, a desired outcome could be a certain weight or level of fitness. An output is what is delivered at the end of a process; for example, "going to the gym" delivers the output "worked out." Once you understand which outcomes you want to create, you can align your daily processes and their subsequent outputs to create them.

The things you do every day, however, are not the point. If you've identified yourself as a pack rat, and part of your goal is to have a tidy home, you may set in motion a process to remove ten things from your home every day. At the end of the first day, ten things are gone, and you feel pretty good about it. The process works: it has successfully delivered the desired output of removing ten things from your home. With all that positive feedback, you keep it up for a month. At the end of the month, you're shocked to find yourself obsessively looking around for things to toss or give away, and as you're looking around, it occurs to you that the house is still not tidy. What went wrong?

It's possible to get so wrapped up in a process and its output that the desired outcome gets lost in the shuffle. If the defined outcome is "a happy marriage" and you kick off a process called "never fight," you might be surprised when your spouse hands you divorce papers and says he or she doesn't know you anymore. If the defined outcome is "weigh 135 pounds," and you're counting visits to the gym but stuffing your face with chocolate ice cream every night . . . well, you get the point.

Most successful outcomes require the convergence of more than one process to achieve. If you want to lose weight, there's the process called "exercise" and there's the process called "diet," but ultimately the measurement that makes a difference is the number of pounds lost, not how many times you went to the gym or how many calories you ate. Your measures should focus on your desired end result, not the steps to get there.

Second, your measurements should be concrete. It's all well and good for a company executive to want the outcome "improve the bottom line," but what exactly does that mean? Is it a 10 percent improvement, or a 300 percent improvement? If your desired outcomes include becoming financially secure, what's the definition of "financially secure," and by when does it need to happen? Without knowing what success specifically looks like, you'll find it hard to establish a measurement system to drive it. The more succinctly you can define your outcome, the more likely you'll be able to apply specific measurements to make it happen.

Lastly, your measures need to be consistent. If you intend to use measurement to accelerate your creation of a certain outcome, then regular measurements of your progress toward that outcome must be taken. Because of our habit of using measurement to judge ourselves, we sometimes shy away from it because we know we won't like the result. Have you ever bypassed the bathroom scale while you were on a diet? Interestingly, it's the measurements we'd prefer not to take that can tell us the most about fixing our game. Letting go of our fear and judgment here, too, gives us the knowledge we need to smooth out the rough patches on our journey.

For example, if you want to feel comfortable when speaking in public, but forget to measure your comfort level when you feel really uncomfortable, it will be difficult for you to use measurement to gain much ground on that specific outcome. Examining those times when you feel uncomfortable can yield incredibly valuable information. Was it the size of the group? The nature of the people in the audience? The setup of the room? The topic? Something you did the night before? By narrowing down the reasons for your discomfort, you can create a plan for handling each of them next time. Without a disciplined approach to the problem, not much is likely to change.

Yes, measurement is a discipline. Like any other discipline, it requires rigorous application. But when your vision begins to come true much sooner than you thought possible, and you realize you're the conductor of your own life symphony, the weight of the conductor's baton in your hand, controlling the tempo, will seem feather light.

REDEFINING YOURSELF VIA MEASUREMENT

When you do decide to start measuring your activities consciously, you should be prepared to change. You won't have to do the changing. It will happen to you. You'll become able to produce results with far less effort. Let me give you an example from quantum physics.

In an experiment conducted by a research team at the University of Illinois at Urbana-Champaign, led by Paul Kwiat, a quantum computer returned a result without even being turned on. A photon entering the computer could choose one of two possible paths, one into the computer and one bypassing it. As we know from the double slit experiment described in chapter 1, a photon can and will take all possible paths. To find out which path the photon took, the researchers repeatedly measured the light down each of the paths to see which way it went. By doing so, they forced the photon to give up its superposition (being on both paths at once) and to appear on one path or the other. When it appeared along the bypass path, it sometimes had the information it would have had if it had passed through the computer. In other words, the photon was able to explore and retain information from a region of space it wasn't actually in, and from a process it hadn't actually triggered   but could have. The *possibility* that it could have triggered it returned the right answer.

In the same way, designing a positive measurement system that supports your amplification process creates a path you *could* have gone down, even if you don't. By establishing a positive measurement system, you change the lens through which you view the expenditure of your time, events, social interactions, and so on. In conversation, your ears will perk up at the hint of a resource that could help you achieve measurement A. While sitting in a seminar, you will write down ideas that could help you reach measurement B. Just as the photon's quantum nature "flirted" with the insides of the computer even when it didn't pass through, so your brain will begin looking for synergies that line up with your measurement system. Once definite targets attached to your vision are established, they will begin to seep into all areas of your life, coloring them.

For example, if physical fitness is part of your vision, you might create the judgment-neutral and positive measure of working out three times a week. Even if you don't actually work out three times a week, you will want to. The establishment of the measure will remind you daily that you've met it or have not. As the days of the week tick by, you'll develop contingency plans. "Well, I didn't get to the gym today, so that means that I will go tomorrow morning, Thursday, and Saturday." If you don't go the next morning, the plan might change to Thursday, Friday, and Saturday mornings. If you don't go Thursday, then either you've blown your measure or your Sunday sleep-in. And the next week it starts all over again, perhaps with a goal of working out four times, since you didn't quite make your goal the week before.

To make the measurement happen, you may find yourself at the gym for an evening workout when historically you've only worked out in the morning. You'll make yourself go to the gym and tell yourself you'll stay only for fifteen minutes, and then end up completing a full workout. You might do something you haven't done for years, like play tennis or drag out your bike and go for a ride. If a friend calls and asks if you want to do something together, you might suggest a physical activity rather than a movie or dinner.

If you were to plot on a graph the number of times you work out during this period, I guarantee you would find yourself going to the gym more or discovering other ways to work out and counting those. As soon as you gave up the measurement, though, the plot line would go through the floor. The measurement itself creates the buoyancy.

That's why I recommend milestone celebrations. When you find yourself meeting or exceeding a measure that you've tied to the realization of your vision, celebrate! Take a positive measurement of achieving the measurement. Celebrate it with the same attention that you give your favorite holiday. Shouldn't there be cake and balloons? Will you take the day off or spend it partying with friends? Is there a special meal that you'll invite someone to share with you? How else will you embed the value of this achievement in your brain?

I mean, *really*. Don't let these special days pass with just a nod, a smile, and a whispered "thank you," or "isn't that great." Treasure them, honor them, and give them your full attention. Here's a good reason why: you have no idea how much time you have left. Two of my closest friends lost their husbands at the ages of forty-eight and fifty-one, one while I was editing this book. All you have is now. Now. Now. Use it to feel proud, grateful, powerful, and happy. Life is short, and we don't even know how short. Now is the time to amp it up!

MEASURE OR METRIC?

When you create a new measure, says Dr. Dean Spitzer in his book *Transforming Performance Measurement*, consider calling it an "indicator" at first. Subjecting a new measure to some testing will help you determine whether it's helpful or not. Once you're confident that the indicator will support your creative process, then it graduates to "measure." Only when you feel that a measure is one of the top measures that will bring your vision to life should you call it a "metric" or "key metric." In the business world, key metrics are also known as key performance indicators. You should have a small collection of these, definitely fewer than ten. I would shoot for three to five. More than that could dilute your attention and reduce your effectiveness.

From time to time, you will find it necessary to give up a metric. If your vision includes the completion of a project, such as the sale of a business, you may establish key metrics to push that objective forward. Once the sale is complete, those metrics can be discarded and replaced with new ones that will drive another part of your vision.

It's also a good idea to review your measures from time to time to see if they're still performing for you and garnering results. An ineffective measure is one that measures the wrong thing.

Perhaps you've fallen back into the pattern of using it to judge yourself, or are using it in some other negative manner. Your measure might report to you your failure to reach a goal more than report your achievement of it, for example. If a measure gets tired, create a new one that will reenergize you.

Finally, a measure might need to be replaced if you've identified it as a key metric but it turns out not to be a driver of the results you want. Let's say that in our physical fitness example, you do get to the gym three times a week, *despite how much you hate it.* While you're there you do a lackluster, underpowered twenty minutes on the treadmill, lift a few weights that are a bit too light for you, and then skedaddle on home. What's wrong with this picture? Does the metric "three times a week" really drive the outcome "more physically fit"? Not in this scenario. Designing a new measure that will challenge you physically in fun ways and inspire you would get you closer to your goal than mechanically going through the motions to achieve your "key" metric. "I will pick and perform three fun physical activities per week" is much more likely to create your desired results — and is even fun to say, given all the alliteration.

When measurement is used as a positive and reinforcing steering tool rather than as a grading tool, it directs your behavior, focuses your attention, clarifies your self-expectations, improves your execution, promotes consistency and self-alignment, improves your ability to make decisions, motivates you, and brings your vision to life faster.

I could use a bit of all that. How about you?

PART II.

APPLYING THE FIVE SECRETS
FROM SCIENCE IN YOUR LIFE

6. AMP UP YOUR WEALTH

Bringing the Buried Treasure to the Surface

MY ROLE MODEL WHEN IT COMES TO CREATING WEALTH is my dear and lifelong friend Katie. Years ago, Katie won a very large sum of money in a state lottery. I absolutely believe that she called that money to her. Here's her diary entry from the day before she won: "Things are starting to happen. I can feel it!" I also have a picture she drew of herself standing with fistfuls of money in front of a wall covered with pictures of the things she was going to do once she had the money.

Before she won, Katie was not living the life of her dreams. In fact, just the opposite: She was divorced, raising a young son, and living on the edge of poverty. She resided in an apartment over a liquor store that she shared with another single mom and her child. She'd dropped out of high school because of difficulties she'd faced as a teenager, so her career prospects seemed limited. Katie needed a miracle — and she knew it. Against this stark, unfriendly, and seemingly hopeless backdrop, Katie managed to create a vision so strong that she caused the universe to move.

I remember the day she called to tell me. She said, quite

casually, "So, what's up with you?" For the next few minutes, I proceeded to rattle off a list of the usual kinds of things we talked about. In retrospect, I can see that list must have killed her.

Finally, I said, "What's up with you?"

That's when Katie said, "I won the lottery."

I said, "No you didn't."

She said, "Yeah, I did."

I said, more insistently, "No, you didn't!"

She said, "Yeah. I did."

I said, "How much?"

She said, "1.2 million dollars."

I think I jumped off the couch then. "You are kidding me!"

"No, I'm not." I could hear her grinning at this point. "I really won."

She had, in fact, won. She had created a miracle in her life. Since then, Katie has attained several degrees, worked in television, done computer animation, moved to the mountains of Colorado, found the man of her dreams, and become an accomplished painter. She's done everything she's wanted to do. If you are lucky enough to attend one of my seminars at which Katie speaks, you will understand why she is so relaxed. Katie has the universe at her fingertips. Now she's working on winning the Powerball lottery. (Current estimated jackpot: $360 million.)

Here's the great truth from this story: You have the abundant universe at your fingertips too. You need only open up to the possibilities.

ACCESSING THE POSSIBILITY

This is the fun part. In this section, you get to build a detailed vision that specifically addresses the financial aspect of your life. If you've always dreamed of a life of comfort and wealth, then creating this vision may seem like an adventure.

For my friend Katie, the visioning process of creating wealth was very important. She envisioned money coming to her easily and without effort, and she imagined how she would spend the money, as if she had already received it. The lottery was one way in which she thought this abundance might come to her, but she was open to the possibility that her request would be delivered through any mechanism the universe chose. So although you may have an idea of how you want wealth to come to you — perhaps by getting a raise or starting a business — for the moment be more like Katie and reserve those specific aspirations for your professional vision, discussed in chapter 7. Right now focus on what it will be like once you've achieved financial bliss.

When you create your vision of wealth, be open first to all possibilities by staying in wave mode, using one of the techniques described in chapter 1 to get there. Once you are in wave mode, consider the following questions in order to launch your thought process.

What Does Being Wealthy Look Like to You?

Is wealth a specific amount of income per year, or a specific amount in the bank? Is it a certain size home, a home in a particular location, or more than one home? Is it having the car of your dreams? Is it being able to get on a plane and go wherever you want, whenever you want? Is it paying for your kids' college education without effort? Maybe you dream of sleeping soundly, no longer troubled by money worries. Maybe with wealth you can comfortably afford a yacht with a captain and an ocean-view penthouse with a dock space. With a little imagination, you can be your own financial visionary.

And since we're on the topic of financial visionaries, I recently went to hear Suze Orman speak in Miami. If you don't know Suze, run to the bookstore today and pick up one of her many books. Suze is an expert at guiding people through the process of taking control of their own money, no matter how meager an amount that might be. At the event I went to, after Suze introduced her new book, *Women and Money*, she invited questions from the audience. The first person at that microphone was one of the few males in the audience, who said, "Suze, save our marriage. Tell my wife that a joint savings account is just as good as or better than a savings account in just her name." I almost fell out of my chair. You've got to be kidding me, I thought. What year is this again?

Suze was not fazed. She'd heard this many times before. She invited the man's wife to the podium, and made this comment to the man: "I'm not going to save your marriage. I'm going to make it ten times better." She turned to the woman next to her.

"How many years have you been married?" she asked.

"Fifty-three years," the woman replied with a smile.

"How long have you wanted a savings account of your own?"

"Forever," the woman replied. The supportive and mostly female audience gasped. (But it gets worse!)

"And," the woman said, "I worked for twenty-five of those years."

Why didn't this woman have a savings account? Because she let someone else tell her how she would run her financial affairs. Her financial dream was simple, but it was about *control*. I pray that she got that account. No, wait! That would mean that her husband *gave* it to her. So what I really pray is that she amped it up and went the next day to open her own account whether he wanted her to or not. Because Suze is right: a marriage in which *both* parties share financial control is a better marriage. If this gentleman falls sick, becomes incapacitated, or dies, will his wife be ready to deal with all the financial fallout? Will she have access to the couple's wealth and be able to protect it? Suze spent the next several minutes describing some of the horrors that have befallen couples in which only one partner had financial empowerment.

Visions of wealth are as individualized as the people who create them. Don't think you must include a specific indicator of wealth if it doesn't resonate with you. Not everybody wants a Jacuzzi. But you better have a savings account. And don't let anybody tell you that you can't have one.

Reverse Troublesome Financial Situations Now

In the financial category particularly, you may find that your goals are about getting rid of financial problems rather than creating financial abundance. You may have a ton of credit card debt, or your retirement may be in question. Don't despair, if so. You can transform these worries through the amplification process.

For example, if your business is in trouble, add to your vision that the business's financial issues are resolved and that it is comfortably — if not ecstatically — in the black. Pandemonium Books & Games is a science fiction and gaming bookstore that recently moved out of Harvard Square in Cambridge, Massachusetts, to a new and much larger location in Central Square. Some unforeseen issues caused the store to close for three months, and the debts began to mount. The store finally opened, but was so far in the red that the future looked bleak. In a flash of brilliance, the owner of the store, Tyler Stewart, reached out electronically to the community that had supported the store for the previous seventeen years and asked them to help by preordering branded T-shirts. He bluntly told his audience that he needed a thousand people to preorder T-shirts, or he would have to "start rolling up the business." Back taxes must be paid! The plea was authentic and down-to-earth, and customers not only ordered the T-shirts but also began pouring into the store's new location to buy things and support the store. In less than two months, the store sold its goal of a thousand T-shirts and was able to keep its doors open.

As you can see, even if you think your financial situation is untenable, there *are* solutions. By allowing that there are, you will be amazed at how the answers begin to come to you or unfold. So don't be afraid to include in your vision of wealth some things you think are completely impossible. As far as I was concerned, it was completely impossible for Katie to win the lottery. Thankfully, my limited thinking didn't have an effect on her outcome!

Add Time Frames to the Financial Situation You Want to Create

For example, where would you like to be financially at the end of this year? At the end of five years? Ten? Create some urgency in your vision by giving yourself deadlines for making your dreams come true. Financial well-being has little value if you intend to achieve it "someday." Be bold! Commit to being financially successful in a short enough time frame that it scares you a little. Having a challenging goal is no detriment.

Leo Burnett, the famous ad executive, once said, "When you reach for the stars, you may not quite get one, but you won't come up with a handful of mud either."[1] I'd rather have stardust than mud in my hand any day. Giving yourself deadlines will propel you toward the stars with at least enough thrust to get you into outer space. The stars are a lot prettier from there, and they look a lot closer. Getting that close to them will give you the inspiration you need to set new goals and new deadlines and keep on amplifying.

Gauge the Emotional Impact of Your Vision

Is your vision compelling enough to motivate you to act? Have you captured the essence of your desires? Does your vision give you a thrill or the chills or a feeling of happy contentedness when you think about it? Is it powerful enough to inspire others to go on this journey with you? How will you feel when you actually have the things or experiences listed in your vision?

Write Down All That You Have Fantasized, Then Fantasize Some More

Take a tour of the Internet to find the details that will make your vision come to life. Visit the bookstore and look through magazines that pertain to your financial vision. All those pictures will help you visualize your desired outcome more powerfully. Give your vision some time to grow and ripen, and then, when it is perfect for plucking, we'll apply some amplification magic to make it a state fair contest winner.

AMP IT UP!

Okay, so now you have your vision, a list of circumstances and material items that describe the financial life of your dreams. It seems to be the perfect picture of your financial life, and everything in it is very important to you. Unfortunately, there's a sad truth I must reveal to you: Your vision is a shadow of what it could be. Your vision is a snapshot. It's not a full-motion video. Your vision is black-and-white, and what you need is Technicolor. You can't see it now, but the fuzzy, out-of-focus thing you just created is like you looking at your future from behind some smudgy glasses — and what you need is lens cleaner. It's time now to make your financial vision even more powerful by making it juicier, bolder, bigger, clearer, and ten times more exciting than it is now. In other words, it's time to *amp it up!*

The following worksheet is designed to be a thought-starter to pump powerful, high-frequency life into your vision of wealth. I also encourage you to go back and apply the twelve steps in chapter 2 specifically to achieve an even more powerful amplification of your vision. When you're finished with this exercise, you'll be able to sense the energy you have created by your thoughts alone. You'll look forward as well as back, and all of a sudden the incredible importance of your actually achieving this thing you've created will become apparent.

AMP UP YOUR WEALTH! WORKSHEET

I'm sure you're not rich enough yet! Let's get you richer. Remember dollars are made out of energy and space, just like everything else, and there's plenty of 'em to go around.

You've already created your wealth vision. Now take your time and really think about the following questions. Use them as inspiration to amp up your vision. The bigger your vision, the more likely you are to make great progress. Reach far!

The first five questions have to do with financial risk. Financial risk is a hot topic, but financially successful people would not be successful without it. The kind of risk you want to take is a calculated risk. I'm obviously not talking about handing a large sum of your money to a stranger who says there's buried treasure in your garden. (Believe it or not, two people fell for that scam here in South Florida recently.)

1. Do you have unused equity in your home? Could you use that equity to buy another income-generating property?
2. Do you have money socked away in a low-earning savings account? Could that money be put to better use and earn you more money?

3. If you own multiple properties and are employed, you may not be taking advantage of some major tax breaks available to you. Would you be willing to quit your job and create income from another source?

4. Would you be willing to go into debt to make your dream come true? What would it take for you to get comfortable with that, if it were necessary? (Or what would it take for you to do it anyway, despite your fear?)

5. Is someone telling you that you can't achieve your financial vision, that you will never achieve your financial goals? Are you willing to break your dependence on her opinion of you, and do it anyway?

Streeeeeccetch that financial dream envelope! We're not looking for quarters in the couch cushions here. We want you and your family to be financially comfortable for the rest of your lives — and more. The following questions will help expand your vision of what wealth looks like.

6. Do you want to leave a large inheritance to your children and grandchildren? How big? Will you leave it in trust? In what month and year will you set up that trust and with what initial deposit?

7. Do you want to teach your children how easy and fun it is to make money? Are you ready to write the lesson plans yet?

8. Is there a local or global charity you could take to great new heights if you were to fund it? Which charity? How much would you like to give them every year? Are there other charities that are or could be

close to your heart, and that would benefit from your giving?

9. Is there a hospital that needs a wing with your name on it? A university?

10. Would you like to establish a family foundation that gives money in perpetuity to causes you define?

11. Is there someone struggling financially that you would like to make sure is always taken care of?

12. What else would you like your money to do for you while you're here or after you're gone?

Are you sure you've put enough money in your vision to go to all the places and have all the experiences you could ever want and to share them with your loved ones? I recommend naming a specific amount, by the way. But before you nail that number down, consider the following.

13. If your goal is to make more money and work less, have you scheduled enough vacations in your calendar year? Are all the accommodations for those vacations top, top notch?

14. How many vacation homes are in your vision? Is that enough?

15. Have you ever wanted to do something really wacky, like go to space? Is that in your vision?

16. Got all those big parties you want to throw? How often do you bring your friends together at your expense? Do you want to establish a regularly scheduled celebration that your invitees can attend weekly or monthly?

17. Is there something you've always wanted to learn how to do? Water-ski? Skydive? Create stained glass

windows? Kite board? Cave dive? Train dolphins?
Do you want to be privately taught by a master?

18. Would you like to have private performances by famous musicians in your palatial home? Other private
performances?

19. Do you have an adequate transportation plan? Heli-
copter? Private plane? Yacht? Limo?

20. I can't *tell* you how important it is that you stop doing
the things you don't like to do. Do you have appro-
priate staff in your vision? Some positions you might
consider adding: chef, butler, valet, nanny, personal
trainer, hairstylist, maid, personal assistant, book-
keeper, pilot, chauffeur, and boat captain.

It hardly matters how much money you have if it makes you unhappy. Here are some questions to help you explore how you want
to feel when your wealth vision comes true, and some possible
paths to get there.

21. Do you want to work more or less? How many days
a week? How many hours per day?

22. Do you want to spend time managing your money
because it's something you enjoy? Or would you prefer to put things on automatic pilot or hire an advisor
to manage your wealth? If you hire someone, how do
you want to feel about that person?

23. Do you need to shed some old frames concerning
money? What new frames would you like to create?

24. What is the primary emotion you would like to feel
each day about your financial situation? What is the
one emotion you no longer want to feel when you
think about money?

25. Are your thoughts focused on what you want to create, or are they focused on what you *don't* want in your life anymore? For example, can you see that if your vision includes eliminating calls from debt collectors, the actions, thoughts, and behaviors that stem from that vision will be much different than if your vision focuses on appreciating the abundance in your life, or having a retirement fund that is way more than adequate? You're not trying to create "no debt collectors." You're trying to create "limitless financial abundance and security." Right?

BELIEF MANAGEMENT

As you saw in chapter 3, there are two types of beliefs: those that put you in growth mode, and those that put you in protective mode. The first propels you toward your vision, and the second pushes it farther away from you. We have both types of beliefs inside us. Sometimes we feel especially aligned with one type of belief or the other.

Before Katie won the lottery, she created what she calls "an air of expectant anticipation," a sense of knowing that the universe is capable of delivering her desired outcome and that in time it will. She used several modalities to affirm her belief, including journaling and drawing, and in that way she aligned herself strongly with her vision. When your whole being is aligned with your beliefs, you become an unstoppable powerhouse of energy and focus.

Now, here's a reminder: aligning your behavior and your beliefs is *easy* and *fun*. Remember when you were a child engaged in a game of pretend? The rest of the world melted away. That towel around your shoulders *was* a plush red velvet cape, and that paper crown on your head *was* bejeweled and made of gold. You could see the castle walls around you, see the horses toss their heads, feel their soft muzzles in your palm. Or maybe for you it was rocket ships, or cowboys and Indians, or "house." Do you remember that when the game was over, interrupted by something like your mom calling you for dinner, there was a moment of disorientation as you shifted back to the "real" world? And all you did to create that castled world was to desire it and give yourself to it completely. You spent time focused on building the image of your world in your mind, and then you lived inside it.

Back then, when you were not so programmed, it was easy to slip in and out of the worlds of your beliefs. Here's a worksheet to help you slip into the world of wealth and align yourself with the knowledge that your financial vision is possible, that it's inevitable, and that you are capable of making it come true.

MY *MAKE IT HAPPEN!* BELIEF CREATION PLAN TO SUPPORT WEALTH

Belief Creation Tools

(For suggestions on using these tools, refer to chapter 3.)

MEDITATION. Quiet your mind by focusing on a phrase, an object, your breath, or the guidance of another, in order to enhance self-awareness.

A PRACTICE OF CONTEMPLATION AND REFLECTION. Use this regular, dedicated time alone to focus on, amplify, and embed particular thoughts and ideas crucial to creating your dream.

VISUALIZATION. Picture in your mind's eye a situation as you dream it can be.

IMMERSIVE PROBLEM SOLVING. Engage in the "doing" of the belief that is being created in order to absorb the belief. (For example, if your new belief is that money comes to you easily, how would you apply this belief in real-world situations?)

THE IMAGINED AUDIENCE. Pretend to relate the story of your success in a public forum, whether you imagine a single confidante or a large group.

BLOGGING. Share the creation of your dream by posting online at least daily using free or paid blogging tools on the Internet to create a public journal of your success.

VLOGGING. Use a video camera to record each online post, as opposed to text. Vlogging can also be done in combination with blogging.

JOURNALING. Create a "success journal" to capture the qualities of your dream life in writing, and update it at least weekly.

PRAYER. Communicate with the deity of your choice, according to the religious tradition of your choice, to make requests regarding the creation of your dream life and to extend gratitude.

PRE-THANKING. Thank the Powers That Be as if your dream creation has already come true. (Which it has; we're just waiting for it to show up here.)

Do you have some belief creation tools that you're already using with great success? Record them here, and use them everywhere in the creation process.

CUSTOM BELIEF CREATION TOOL #1 _____

_____

CUSTOM BELIEF CREATION TOOL #2 _____

_____

CUSTOM BELIEF CREATION TOOL #3 _____

_____

Your Belief Creation Commitment

Choose no more than five tools from the Belief Creation Plan above, and use them to generate a powerful state of belief about the creation of your dream life. Set a schedule for using them and commit to it.

TOOL	M	T	W	TH	F	S	SU
JOURNALING			X			X	

You spent many years constructing the beliefs that got you where you are today. Some of them are serving you, and some are holding you back. You can amp up the power of your current positive beliefs about yourself and your situation by creating new supporting or dominant beliefs to go along with them and by practicing those beliefs using the tools described here.

DECOHERE IT

Decoherence is all about interacting with your environment in powerful ways to create the outcomes you want, rather than following the same old paths of probability to create the same old outcomes. I call the latter "probability fragility." It's our tendency to rely on evidence that confirms our usual way of being; at the same time, we generally don't seek out disconfirming evidence, or evidence that our usual way of being is based on flawed, uninformed, or unexamined assumptions. In bringing your vision of wealth to life, look hard for the disconfirming evidence. What evidence have you not yet taken into account that might directly conflict with your beliefs about creating personal wealth?

For example, you may believe you are somehow limited in your ability to create greater abundance for yourself. Your confirming evidence for such a belief is that you are unhappy or unsatisfied with your financial situation and yet have not been able to rectify it so far. If you could flip that around, you might realize that you have built a financial life that fits in with your expectations of yourself and your world. And not only *your* expectations but also the expectations of the people around you. You may give more credence to the opinions of friends and family than to actual fact.

In reality, people from *all* walks of life and *all* financial situations have created enormous abundance for themselves. This disconfirming evidence supports the fact that this ability is available to you as well, despite your current beliefs or the input you are receiving from others.

So, what evidence have you *not* thoroughly looked at — or chosen to ignore — that says you *are* destined to have a life of abundance? For example, if your goal is to be a multimillionaire, and your current income is nowhere near that, what role models can you find who rose from low incomes to multimillionaire status? If you can't think of any, I'll give you one: Suze Orman, the financial visionary I mentioned earlier in this chapter. Suze walked away from college without finishing her degree. She was a waitress until she was thirty years old. She dressed inappropriately for job interviews. And now she's worth $37 million. If Suze Orman did it, so can you. Can't relate? Of course you can't! The nature of disconfirming evidence is that it feels a lot less like the truth than what you think you already know. For this reason, it's essential that you look for as much of this type of evidence as you can find, and that you weigh it even more heavily when forming your beliefs and taking action than the confirming evidence you already have in hand.

Another way to influence your environment is by repetitive action. My mom, who has no financial background, began watching Bloomberg Television and MSNBC's financial programming. When I say she watches it, I mean she watches for hours every day. She videotapes her favorite shows when she will miss them and then watches them later. She watches it when she's running on the treadmill, and she writes down daily stock prices from the scrolling tickers. Yes, while she's running. Mom still thinks she doesn't know what she's doing, but her portfolio regularly outperforms the stock market. I guess it doesn't matter what she believes then, does it?

Katie, my friend the lottery winner, did her part to decohere the present by regularly buying lottery tickets. The lottery — of all things — is just a game of probabilities, is it not? Katie persisted in her regular participation and capitalized on that numbers game, and your persistent action in the direction of your dreams will produce results too.

Another way to decohere your financial present into the desired patterns of your financial future is to take action to surround yourself with the trappings of your vision. Do you imagine sipping champagne at a fancy local club, but end up drinking beer in front of the TV? Time to go out for a glass of champagne. Are any of your current friends role models in the creation of abundance? See if you can acquire some new friends who can help you learn and grow in this area. Do your attempts to create abundance feel dry and unrewarding? You can do what my friend Stephanie did.

She created a reward system for herself by putting aside a small portion of what she earned, and designated it as mad money. She tells me that doing so changed her whole perspective on abundance, making it much more enjoyable. It might just be enough for a Starbucks Venti coffee in some cases, or it might be enough for a pair of new shoes. In the "Room for the Future Worksheet" that follows, you'll get the chance to write down your habitual actions that are not serving your vision and the replacements that will decohere them.

Finally, dwell on the financial vision you have created for yourself. Use the tension between your desired outcome and today's reality to support changes in your behaviors.

ROOM FOR THE FUTURE WORKSHEET

In this exercise, list actions that are part of your regular repertoire, but that won't support your financial vision. Then list new actions you will use to decohere the ones that aren't working for you. I've given you an example here too.

I DON'T SUPPORT MY FINANCIAL VISION WHEN I . . . make late payments on my credit cards, because the late fees are outrageous (and make me angry, and my vision doesn't include anger),

SO INSTEAD I WILL . . . put a reminder in my calendar to send a check one week before each credit card payment is due.

I DON'T SUPPORT MY FINANCIAL VISION WHEN I . . . _____

_____ ,

SO INSTEAD I WILL . . . _____

_____ .

I DON'T SUPPORT MY FINANCIAL VISION WHEN I ... _____

_____ ,

SO INSTEAD I WILL ... _____

_____ .

I DON'T SUPPORT MY FINANCIAL VISION WHEN I ... _____

_____ ,

SO INSTEAD I WILL ... _____

_____ .

APPLY THE INVERSE ZENO EFFECT

Today you have already done at least one good thing toward your financial vision. You may not have planned to, but you did. For example, maybe you had a salad for lunch. Besides being one of the cheaper items on the menu, a salad is also very healthy for you, and I can assure you that today's salad and all the salads before and after it will help stem the tide of medical bills that you will accumulate over your lifetime. Same thing for that run you took this morning. Similarly, you saved additional money if you got your car's oil changed. Keeping your car healthy saves you repair bills. The great client meeting you had did a lot for you too. Even if you didn't walk out the door with any business today, your professionalism and friendliness left an impression that you will be able to go back and collect on later. Or did you curse yourself in the car for screwing up and not getting the business?

How and when you measure your financial progress will either slow you down or speed you up. There are three major financial areas to which you can apply the inverse Zeno effect: debt management, savings plans, and revenue generation.

Zeno Your Debt

One of the most crippling dilemmas for those trying to improve their financial situation is credit card debt. When I separated from my husband, we owed eighteen thousand dollars on a single MasterCard. Collectors were calling me every day because of a vacation that my husband had charged on an American Express card, which we were unable to pay back. Because our bills were all being sent to my husband's office, it was some time before I discovered that we were paying our credit cards with credit lines. I had at least three department store cards, although those started getting cut off due to nonpayment as well. My credit score was abysmal, and no one was willing to give me any more credit. Thank God. I was forced to start paying cash for everything. It saved my life. I paid off all my debt, I reestablished good credit, and now wealth is abundant in my life. You can do it, too.

If you have multiple credit cards with balances, you can pay them off most quickly by focusing first on the card with the lowest balance. Pay more than the minimum on that card, and pay the minimum on the rest until the first card is paid off. Then start working on the card with the next highest balance, and so on. Some suggested places to notice and measure your progress that will activate the inverse Zeno effect and accelerate your efforts include:

- Every payment you make on the primary card that is more than the minimum.
- Every card you pay off by using this method. (This also qualifies for a milestone celebration, discussed in chapter 5.)
- Looking at your credit card statements to see which card has the lowest balance. (Yes. Just looking. Remember how powerful observation is?)

- Moving from making late payments to on-time payments.
- Putting the primary card in a drawer rather than in your wallet.
- Cutting up the cards and throwing them away. (Good for a milestone celebration.)
- Paying cash for an item for which you would normally throw down a card.
- Refusing to open a department store credit account, even though you will get 10 percent off. (Particularly given today's "inactivity fees." Yes, department stores are now charging you for not using their cards. Beware!)

As you can see, there are all kinds of ways to measure how you are managing credit card debt that reinforce your progress toward your vision. The kinds of measurements that will stimulate the Zeno effect rather than its inverse, and slow you down, include:

- Calculating the number of months or years you have been struggling to pay off this debt.
- Reminding yourself every time you open a bill that you are an idiot for wracking up this much debt.
- Counting the number of pairs of shoes in your closet, all of which you bought on credit, and cursing yourself for it.
- Totaling up your credit card debt, and calculating how much interest you might have earned if it were in a savings account. And reminding yourself how dumb you are.

I recently interviewed Karolina Linares, author of *Use Cash to Buy It!*, a step-by-step guide for getting out of credit card debt.

Karolina is an expert on this topic, since she herself once had fourteen thousand dollars in credit card debt, which was about half her annual salary at the time. It took her five years to pay it off. She pointed out to me that it's not just about the money. A person's whole lifestyle has to change to pay off a large debt. Values need to be reexamined. Recreational activities must be curtailed or eliminated altogether. Even decisions about groceries have to be thought out. The emotional impact can be debilitating. Karolina helped herself stay on track by measuring her progress. "I kept really good track of how I was doing," she said. "You have to sit back and take a look at yourself and say, 'You know what? I *am* making progress, and I *am* doing this.' You have to pat yourself on the back and feel enlightened that you're doing a good thing in your life rather than dwelling on it, thinking you need to be punished."

If you are under the burden of a large debt, the only thing I can recommend that you buy is Karolina's book. And then do everything she says, including patting yourself on the back frequently for the progress you're making.

POSSIBILITY TIP

Remember, any measurement that reinforces the negative actions you have taken instead of the positive ones will slow you down or stop you altogether.

Zeno Your Savings

Pay yourself first, pay yourself first, pay yourself first. Every time you pay yourself first, take a measurement. Do you have a regular before-tax paycheck deduction that goes to a savings account? If you do, give yourself points! (You get to decide how many.) Is there a way to cut your expenses so that you will have money left over at the end of the month to put away? For example, you could strike the word *Venti* from your vocabulary. (For those of you who, like me, are not coffee drinkers, a Venti is the largest size coffee you can buy at Starbucks. I had to look it up on the Web. In some parts of the country that Starbucks hasn't penetrated yet, you can substitute the word *grandissimo*.)

If you do stop ordering expensive coffees, take a measurement! Did you forgo a coffee today but buy a pair of shoes? Still take that positive measurement. You took an action in the direction of your dreams. Yes, you also took one that didn't help very much, but it's okay to give yourself credit for picking an action and sticking to it. You're going to mess up periodically. As long as you keep taking actions that point in the direction of your financial vision, and as long as you keep that vision alive in your mind, *and* as long as you keep taking measurements in the right places, you will be able to overcome those occasional slipups. And hey, sometimes life throws you a curveball. Your car breaks down, your bathroom springs a leak, you forgot about the insurance down payment, and so forth. Your commitment to taking action on your dreams, *actually taking action*, and then giving yourself credit for it, will allow you to overcome all of life's unexpected pitches.

The size of the action is immaterial. Let's say you've come to the end of the month, and you're still not rich. Well, okay, let's say that you didn't achieve your savings goal (which I assume is large, since we're into large visions here). Take a moment and record some of the actions you did take during the month that were consistent with the realization of your vision. Did you skip some pleasures that ordinarily you would have spent money on? For example, did you pack your lunch more often, or choose a less expensive item on the menu, or order a bar brand vodka instead of Grey Goose? Did you set up your automatic paycheck deduction?

Did you review your financial vision during the month? Did you practice at least *some* of your belief creation exercises? Any action you took counts. Record it.

If you look back at the month and you find it's a barren wasteland devoid of any attempts to save money whatsoever, then I can offer you only one thing: a twenty-four-hour reprieve. Within twenty-four hours of making this discovery, run down to the ATM. Make a deposit into your savings account. Twenty dollars, five, a hundred . . . whatever you can afford. There. Now you've saved some money.

Too complicated? Then pull out a credit card bill that's on the verge of being late, write a check, and put it in your mailbox. There. You saved a late fee.

Haven't even established a savings account? Find a slot on your calendar and make yourself an appointment to git-r-done, as the comedian Larry the Cable Guy would say. And then record the fact that you took some action.

Zeno Your Revenue

This section is about income, but not just about your paycheck. It's about the revenue that you might generate from your own small business. It's about the income you might generate from your real estate holdings. You might be very good at investing in the stock market, or you could learn how to be. You *can* establish multiple streams of income, and I have to tell you: that phrase was added to my vocabulary by Robert Allen, author of *Multiple Streams of Income*. He's written many other books, by the way, and in my book, he's the king when it comes to getting it done. Much of the way I conduct my business today is based on principles I learned from him.

And yet I know that a lot of what Robert Allen teaches still seems far-fetched to most people. It's hard for people to imagine that they can build a website, send out some newsletters, and make money. The thought of buying another piece of real estate by taking a loan against the equity they have in their own house seems terrifying.

But there are important reasons for exploring other sources of income and other investment options. The volatility of the stock market is one. We all love those stories of the grandma who started investing in FedEx stock, lo those many years ago, and upon her death donated two million dollars to a local university, but we may not be living in such times now.

The fact that we probably can't rely on our employers to keep us around indefinitely is another factor. Corporate fraud that might disappear our pensions, the uncertainty of Social Security, and the fact that in all probability, we are going to live much longer than our parents and grandparents: all these things require that we change it up a bit. In the years to come, we're all going to have to learn more about investing our money, diversifying those investments, and growing what we've got faster and harder. This learning process can be exciting, and the first step you take toward your own financial independence will make you feel like a million bucks.

Whatever you choose, whether it's a decision to monetize a hobby on the side, go into business for yourself, amp up the results you're currently getting from your business, begin to invest in real estate, or take your career to the next level, you will be able to accelerate your progress toward these goals by applying the inverse Zeno effect. Here are some tips for accelerating the generation of revenue:

- **START NOW.** Do not wait. Every moment, every day, every month that goes by without action on your part is a lost opportunity to access the unlimited abundance available to you and make your fiscal dreams come true.

- **TAKE ACTION.** Any action. Buy some books. Read them. Do some research online. Write a plan. Begin it. Tinker with the tools you might use to bring your revenue-generation plan to life. Start sending the pebbles down the hill that will trigger your avalanche.
- **MEASURE YOUR ACTIONS.** Write them down. Record the story of how you started down the path toward wealth. Each measurement will serve as a catalyst and reinforcement of the transformation of your financial life.
- **USE THE GRID.** Talk to your friends and colleagues about the possibilities. Ask for their advice. Use them as guinea pigs. Ask them who you need to know. Get them to introduce you. Invite them to go with you to the educational seminars you must attend to fulfill your financial dreams. Invite them to be your customers. Ask for their referrals.
- **ELIMINATE DRAG.** There are elements of your life that can distract you from the journey to your financial destination. There are external factors creating drag on your forward motion, yet you continue to tolerate them. What are they? They might include irresponsible boyfriends or girlfriends, salespeople in your own business generating mediocre results, or a family member who somehow never seems to have his financial feet under him. You may also be generating internal factors yourself: for example, your own toxic attitude toward your place of work. Or perhaps you have a long-standing habit of psychologically beating yourself up, and when you do, you find it difficult to be productive. You know what these factors in your own life look like. Your continued attention to,

and tolerance of, them will act as a drag on your journey to your dreams. Releasing the things that slow you down may seem impossible. But you know what my take is on that: everything is possible. If you first make it your goal to just lessen the impact of the difficulty, rather than eliminate it completely, you'll find some ways to lighten your load. And lightening your load will make your life easier and more fun. You can find some impact reducers in the "Resources" section of my website.

OPENING THE TREASURE CHEST

Whatever your original vision of wealth looked like, it should now be a lot shinier and more colorful. Hopefully, it's also now too big to stick in your bottom dresser drawer and forget about. Your new beliefs about wealth have prompted you to construct both an investment plan and strategies to take those beliefs to the world and make them come true. Finally, you've been given the controls to create your world of abundance as quickly or as slowly as you want. (I hope you picked "quickly." I'd like us all to show up at the same big, extravagant parties. We'll do it at my house first.)

And there's still so much more. We've touched on only one area of your life so far. Next, we'll explore the way you'd like to spend your time pursuing a chosen occupation. We'll dig into your passions, your strengths, and the best ways to create more fun and joy through their application.

7. AMP UP YOUR CAREER

Maximizing Your Chosen Pursuit

MY FRIEND KEVIN IS A FIREMAN. He has always dreamed of being a fireman, ever since he was a little kid. But it's not something he ever mentioned to me until 2006, when I was working for a newspaper and he was working in cable TV advertising and we were both in our midforties. The road Kevin took to get to the career of his dreams was a long and winding one, the first left turn of which was the divorce of his parents when he was only twelve.

Kevin's mother, Eva, was a diagnosed schizophrenic, which made for a difficult marriage. When Kevin's father filed for divorce, he demanded and got custody of all three kids; Kevin was the youngest. Later, feeling guilty at leaving Eva all alone, he remanded custody of Kevin back to his ex-wife. Eva continued to struggle with her mental illness, but then became physically ill as well, with uterine cancer. At sixteen, Kevin had no choice but to drop out of high school and go to work pumping gas in order to help support his mom. His dream career was quickly forgotten.

His dreams instead became about how he could work only two jobs and still make the same money that he did while working three. Then later, after he had reached that goal, he dreamed of having just one job while still making the money he made working two. He certainly never thought about retirement, or a pension, or designing a career. His goal was simply forward motion, a mantra he has used throughout his life. And so went the next thirty years, he told me. He lived the best he could by always maximizing his current opportunities and looking for better ones.

When Kevin and I met in 2000, we both worked in the same division of a large corporation. He ran sales and I ran operations. I remember him being very angry then. Having separated from his wife a couple of years earlier, he was going through a difficult divorce, and he had two young daughters to worry about. Kevin was frustrated with the bureaucracy at work, set up by a remote corporate headquarters staff, which was compounded by the bureaucracy of a local corporate staff. All he wanted was *forward motion*, but the controls were not always in his hands — and his frustration was palpable.

Then he got sick. At a routine physical, Kevin and his doctor spoke again about a lump on his neck. Kevin had mentioned it during his physical a year earlier, but at the time his doctor had said, "Don't worry about it." This year, the lump was still there, and it was bigger, and now the doctor was worried. Kevin's tests revealed that he had papillary thyroid cancer, and his doctor assured him that this was the "good" kind of thyroid cancer, with twenty-year survivor rates, instead of five. The doctor advised surgery, radiation, and thyroid hormone suppression therapy. "Piece of cake," said the doctor.

But it wasn't. Kevin had a horrible time with the treatment. The medication was so powerful that he found it difficult to function. Some eighteen months later, he couldn't tolerate the medication anymore. He said to his doctor — a new one this time — "We have to back off the meds. I can't work. I can't take care of my kids." The doctor agreed to reduce the dosage. Four months later, Kevin had seventeen tumors in his neck and found himself back on the operating table. Lying in recovery, in so much pain it made him cry, he thought to himself, "I can't live *with* the medication, and I can't live *without* it. *Now* what?"

The answer for Kevin was physical fitness. Before he got ill, Kevin had been a category 3 bike racer, which means he'd raced in more than twenty-five races. Two years before the recurrence of his cancer, Kevin's sister had given him Lance Armstrong's book *It's Not About the Bike*. If you're unfamiliar with Lance or his book, it's the story of a bike racer who overcame testicular cancer (which had spread to his lungs and brain) and then went on to win the Tour de France, the most grueling race in biking, seven times in a row.

Kevin had never read the book. Lying at home recovering, he accidentally rediscovered the book under the couch and read it in one day. It was a life-changing day. He got himself a biking coach and a physical trainer, and got back in the business of getting fit. He started to feel better. The stronger he got, the easier it was to tolerate his medication. Soon, he was able to tolerate it at the full dosage without the chronic effects he'd experienced previously.

Kevin says that Lance Armstrong taught him about warfare: how to battle his disease rather than giving up. A second book, by the late Joseph Cardinal Bernardin, *The Gift of Peace*, taught him about conducting spiritual warfare. "This book helped me prepare to die, but more important, it centered me on how to really live."

The Kevin that I met again, years after working together, was a different Kevin, someone more at peace, more accepting, more at ease with himself. As we worked on a project between his company and mine, he revealed his childhood dream and told me that he was taking courses at the firefighting academy. The coursework was difficult, particularly on top of a full-time job. The physical exercises were grueling, especially for Kevin, who is on a lifetime course of debilitating medication and not exactly a spring chicken like many of the other candidates. But his desire to see his vision come true was so strong that he passed the coursework and the exams with flying colors.

He told me later how he finally began to amplify his dream into reality. It had started the summer before we had begun to work together again. He was feeling better physically, but was really unhappy at work. He was spending a lot of time reevaluating his position on the planet and deciding what to do next. He thought, "If I could teach my kids to follow their dreams, I'd be a successful dad." So he started delivering his dream speech — again — to his two daughters, as they were driving around in the car one day.

Their response shocked him. They said, "Well, you're not going after your dream, Dad, so why should we?" Ouch. Kevin made excuses, saying that he was too old to be a fireman, that he wouldn't be able to make enough money, and so on. As he listened to himself, he realized that the only way he would ever teach this important lesson to his girls would be through action, not speech making. He promised them — and himself — that he would look into it.

Shortly afterward, he and the girls were having dinner in a restaurant together. Sitting a few tables away were two firefighters. His children encouraged him to go talk to them. Kevin said, "Okay. I'll go ask them if they think I'm too old."

"Hell, no!" said one of the firemen. "We just hired a fifty-year-old guy." Kevin came back to the table and made his girls another promise: "I'm gonna do it."

As you know from the top of this chapter, Kevin did it, and so far, he has two favorite stories about being a fireman. The first is about an elderly woman who accidentally pooped on him as he lifted her out of the shower. He says that despite it being the low point of his career as a fireman to date, it was still *way* better than when he used to get crapped on in the corporate world.

The second story is about a woman who went into ventricular fibrillation shortly after Kevin and his partner arrived on the scene. Kevin remembers hooking her up to a heart monitor and pointing out the wacky pattern on the machine to his partner. He looked into the woman's eyes and could see that she was losing consciousness. Her eyes rolled back into her head. Her heart stopped, and she stopped breathing. In other words, she died. Following procedure, Kevin placed a breathing bag over her mouth and nose and began squeezing it regularly to force air into her lungs. His partner pressed the shock paddles to her chest and applied a shock in an attempt to restart her heart.

"All of a sudden, her eyes went *bink*!" Kevin said. "It scared the life out of me! She pushed me off of her. She started talking. As we say, she was 'conscious, alert, and oriented.' We brought her back to life. There isn't another feeling like that in the world."

At one point in our conversation I told him I thought he was courageous. Kevin bowed his head for a moment and then looked me in the eye. "I don't feel courageous," he said. "I feel awake. I feel 'conscious, alert, and oriented.' I've never been happier in my entire life."

Kevin says money is very tight. He's not sure how much time he has left. But he's finally living his dream. If you still have any questions about how happy he is, then you should also know that every once in a while I get a voice mail that consists of only a firetruck's siren wailing, its horn blowing, and Kevin in the background giggling like an idiot.

ACCESSING THE POSSIBILITIES

You may have had a dream since childhood about a particular career, one that you've never allowed yourself to have. Or you may have developed your dream as an adult. Or you may have no clue what you'd like to do, except that you're sure that what you're doing now ain't it.

Kevin was lucky to go back and retrieve his dream from childhood. But he was even luckier that the circumstances in his life opened him up to that possibility again. More fortunate still, he had the courage to stop listening to the Tribe and begin an amplification process that turned it into reality.

When I was a kid, I wanted to be a marine biologist, a geologist, or an archeologist. I loved the sciences, read copious amounts of science fiction, and loved the idea of discovering something no one else had. My mom objected to all of my choices because "you can't make good money in those fields." (I now know that I can make good money in just about *any* field, but this was then.) She said, "Be a systems analyst. They make good money, and they need women in that field!"

Mom was all about being independent. She wanted me to be able to take care of myself, because a good career — and the good money that goes with it — was the one thing she didn't have when she and my father were divorced. She didn't want me to learn the hard way, as she had.

To her suggestion that I become a systems analyst, I said, "Uhhhhh . . . okay." I got a two-year degree in computer science, which taught me that I didn't want to be a computer programmer. (Actually, it took me another year of study to be sure.) I switched to a business focus, and all the lights came on. I was able to apply all the great technological knowledge and training in logic I'd received in my computer science classes to the world of business. My love of discovery has kept me on the cutting edge of business management and technology ever since, and now I've come full circle, to studying the sciences again.

Do I still want to be an archeologist, a marine biologist, or a geologist? Not really. Too much sunscreen. Did I know when I was a teenager why I was so passionate about those professions? Not remotely. It took me twenty-five years to figure it out. Not that I haven't been doing what I'm passionate about all these years; I just didn't know what was driving me. Now I do, and I can consciously apply my passions to any endeavor I embark on. So if you have no idea what you're passionate about, please know that you're not alone. And don't worry. The amplification process can get you connected.

Whether you call it a career, a profession, an occupation, or an avocation, what we're talking about in this chapter is your chosen pursuit. You may want to turn a beloved hobby into a full-time career. Your vision might be of rising to the top of the company you work for now, or growing your small business. Or maybe you still need to match yourself up to a dream career.

If you're in the latter category, and you're not quite sure what you would like to pursue, the next steps are for you. If you already have a dream career in mind, you can skip this part.

What Do I Want to Do?

As hard as it may be to believe, many of us don't really know what we want to do with our lives. There are too many choices. For the young and undecided person, it's often easier not to pick for as long as possible and to take the least resistant path to a job. For the middle-aged, the risk and perceived difficulty associated with shifting gears frightens us and prevents us from spending time exploring and nailing down our desires. And God forbid we should be wrong. Then we'd have to do it all over again! By making the decision that you do want to know what your dream pursuit is, and that you're going to find out, you will give yourself permission to spend time thinking and dreaming about it and will open yourself to the possibilities available to you.

Once you've decided to explore your career choices, innumerable tools are available to help you. Here are some suggestions:

1. **READ BOOKS THAT HELP YOU FIND OUT ABOUT YOU.** One of the books that profoundly influenced my ability to discover my passions was *Now, Discover Your Strengths* by Marcus Buckingham. *The Passion Test* by Janet and Chris Attwood is designed to do the same. A quick search for "dream career" on Amazon.com turns up a long list of books by authors who all could have something special to bring to your discovery process.

2. **SEARCH THE INTERNET.** A website online right now called CareerPerfect.com offers tests that will help you catalog your "career inventory": skills, interests, and values. VocationVacation.com offers a variety of vacations that let you test-drive over 125 different careers. You can find other, similar websites by searching for "dream career" on the search engine of your choice.

3. **EXPLORE YOUR CHILDHOOD.** What games of pretend did you play as a child? What were some of your favorite experiences? In what activities were you most engaged or at peace? By matching up what you know now with what you loved then, a new career path may become evident.

4. **EXPLORE YOUR DAILY LIFE.** What are your favorite things to do today? What parts of your current job do you really love? What parts of it really turn you off? When do you feel like you've really accomplished something? What about yourself makes you most proud? The answers to all these questions may hint at your dream career.

5. **SHARE YOUR QUEST WITH OTHERS.** Visit with someone you know who shares your interests and values and really loves his or her job. Maybe you'd love it too. If you want to stay with your company but do something else, have a conversation with someone in the human resources department to discuss your options. Make a list of people who are already doing what you'd like to do, and ask to speak to them about their careers.

6. **HIRE A COACH.** Life, business, and career coaches can help you choose a career destination and get started. If you want someone to help you brainstorm your options, create a plan, and provide feedback and guidance in executing it, a coaching relationship could be for you.

Once you've chosen your dream pursuit, the first step to amplifying it into reality is to define it succinctly. Here are some steps to get your vision firmly planted.

WRITE IT DOWN. Describe the career you have chosen in as much detail as you can. Is it a job located nearby, or an assignment in another state? Is it a day job, a night job, or an "anytime I want" job? Is it outdoors or indoors? What is the pace of your days? What activities make up your typical day? Do you see a lot of people each day, or do you work mostly alone? How much money are you making? How are you affecting others?

CATALOG THE EMOTIONAL IMPACT OF YOUR DREAM CAREER. As you imagine yourself engaged in your chosen pursuit, how does it make you feel? List the most important and valuable emotions you want to regularly experience in your profession. Does the vision of your dream career light you on fire? You may still be feeling some fear about embarking on this new career adventure, but put that aside for now and instead focus on the emotional state you will create by allowing yourself to spend your time in an activity that has value for you. Once you're in your dream career, you will look back on your uncertainty and smile.

SET A DEADLINE. When do you want to be firmly ensconced in your dream career? Imagine the moment that you say good-bye to your old profession and begin your new one. Can you imagine yourself walking out the door of your company for the last time? Or selling your business for the price you'd hoped to? How much time do you want to give yourself to research your options, develop a strategy, and plan the change? Set a deadline that's not so far away that it won't drive your action today. Really consider how much time you'll need to take courses, train a successor, raise money, build a website, or whatever other preparatory steps you believe are necessary, and set the deadline as close as you can. There's no disadvantage in getting to your dream career sooner rather than later. Knowing your time frame will make your progress measurable and help you apply the inverse Zeno effect.

AMP IT UP!

Climbing the ladder. Getting to the top. It's one of the most popular career visions around. In my career, I have been promoted about a dozen times — and that was only during the years that I wasn't self-employed. If your goal is to advance through the ranks of your current organization with rocket speed, there are some specific things you can do to make yourself more promotable. After analyzing my own history, I've narrowed down the factors in my promotability:

1. VISUALIZING THE ANSWERS TO BUSINESS PROBLEMS. I designed an answer in my head and brought the vision to my boss, who gave me permission — sometimes all you need — to bring the vision to life. Often, along with that permission came a raise and a title.

2. **AMPING IT UP.** Sometimes the problems came to me. On several occasions, a boss asked me if I wanted to manage a project or take over a department. The right answer in such cases is — yes! I was able to create higher visibility for myself in those organizations, which propelled my career forward. Don't think I wasn't scared. Some of those projects were pretty big. But my bosses had confidence I could do it, and so I accepted both the responsibility and the risk.

3. **HAVING OPINIONS.** Wallflowers don't get promoted. They don't succeed as entrepreneurs. Fast career movers must have firm beliefs about themselves, their capabilities, and the work they do. Bringing a clear and different voice to the party will make you stand out. But also be prepared to be wrong and to be flexible if the organization decides that your opinions are not important at the moment. A company can do only so many things at one time, and unless you run it you won't always be the one deciding.

4. **NETWORKING.** If you have a business goal to achieve, there's nothing more valuable than creating relationships across an organization, at your level and above and below you. Also create relationships outside the organization, via associations, clients, friendly competitors, and companies with complementary products or services. By creating a strong network, you'll build up social capital you can call on to create success.

5. **CREATING MEASURABLE RESULTS.** If you can't measure it, it pretty much doesn't count. Whether it's reducing the number of errors in a process, or making sales goals, or getting a better response to a marketing campaign,

you should know three things: (1) Where did you start from? Set a baseline. (2) What does success look like? Set a goal. (3) What must you do to get from the baseline to the goal? Set milestones. If you're not making the milestones, you can reconfigure, correct the process, or give up the goal. If you don't measure what you do, you won't know if your projects are successful, and no one will be able to give you credit for them.

As you may have figured out, the five factors I just outlined are essentially the same five steps of the amplification process that I listed earlier: creating the vision, amping it up, believing, leveraging the environment, and measuring correctly. You can also apply this interpretation of the amplification process to your own business by bringing your vision and opinions to your clients, taking on their problems as if they were your own, delivering measurable results for them, and creating strong relationships as a result. I used these techniques in the first business I started and grew it from nothing to $1 million in annual revenue. You can accomplish the same results and much, much more if you allow yourself to dream big.

AMP UP YOUR CAREER! WORKSHEET

This first set of questions is about taking strategic risks to turn your dream career into reality. If you want to create mobility in your career, you'll likely have to start doing something different. How far are you willing to go to bring your dream to life?

1. Would you leave your current place of employment to better your situation?

2. Could you have a conversation with your boss, the human resources department, or the leader of another division to ask for a specific new opportunity?

3. Would you be willing to give up your job and go back to school full-time to make yourself eligible for a new career and accelerate the realization of your vision?

4. Would you be willing to raise money for a new business and leave your day job? Or raise money to take your current business to the next level?

5. If you don't know what specific steps will get you to your goal, are you willing to ask someone who has already accomplished what you want to accomplish to be your mentor?

6. Would you invest in a career, life, or business coach to accelerate the realization of your vision?

Now, let's imagine for just a minute that you can create the ultimate situation for yourself, in which you have achieved perfect career fulfillment. (Because of course you can.) The following questions will help expand your vision of what the perfect job looks like.

7. If your vision includes getting a raise, how much will it be? Have you envisioned doubling, tripling, or even quintupling your income?

8. If you have a team, how many people are on it? How do you feel about them?

9. Are you your own boss, or are you working for someone else, who truly inspires you and makes you feel good?

10. Do you travel the world first-class on behalf of your chosen pursuit, or does everyone come to you?

11. Do you wear jeans or shorts while you work, or do you have a stylish, tailored, high-end wardrobe from all the best designers?

12. Do you work out of your home or have a fabulous corner office?

13. Do you start your work at eight in the morning? Or do you go to the gym first? Or perhaps you hang out at home with the kids for a while and show up at ten?

14. Does your work affect the community or world in tangible ways?

15. What things will you stop doing in order to focus on creating the career of your dreams?

16. On a scale of one to ten, one being easy and ten being extremely challenging, where does your dream work fall?

17. Are you famous and in the spotlight, or are you content with other rewards for your efforts?

18. Does your work help others fulfill their dreams, or do you want to teach others to do what you do?

Here are some questions to help you more clearly visualize how your chosen pursuit influences the way you feel every day.

19. Do you feel passion in your daily work life? Does time seem to fly because you're so engrossed in what you do?

20. Are your clients, coworkers, and/or bosses grateful to you for your contributions?

21. Is feeling a sense of pride and accomplishment important to you?

22. Are you grateful for being able to do exactly what you love?

23. How do you feel when things don't go exactly right? How would you like to feel?
24. If you could experience one particular emotion more than any other during the workday, what would it be?
25. Do you feel held back by one variable or another and unable to achieve what you want? How could you let that go?

BELIEF MANAGEMENT: A CAUTIONARY TALE

The thing about Teresa was that she was mad. It showed in the way she cared for herself — she smoked, she was overweight, and, from the look of her pasty complexion, she was eating the wrong things. And it showed in the way she dealt with her daily work life.

At meetings, she was bound to speak up. And when she did, you could be sure that her comments would be negative, belligerent, dripping with cynicism and sarcasm, and sometimes outright abusive. Do you know somebody like this? Once she spoke up, everybody else shut up. There was no arguing with her. She'd thought about her positions long and hard, and she had a string of reasons why she was right and the rest of the team — including me, her boss's boss — were wrong. Why risk exposing ourselves to all that anger? Why make ourselves the target? Needless to say, it was difficult to have a productive meeting if Teresa was involved.

Which was a shame. Because Teresa was smart. She had a lot of experience in what she did and a lot of technical knowledge as well. I longed to get the best out of Teresa without also always getting the worst. But everything she knew was attached to her internal framework indicating that everything was wrong with our company. You couldn't separate the two. We, the company's officers and managers, were all idiots, as far as she was concerned, and there was no way to convince her otherwise. Not only were we all incredibly stupid, but we were all out to screw her — and the rest of the staff — as well. She felt that the officers were all becoming rich at the expense of the little people, folks like her and her peers.

Teresa had turned our workplace into a toxic environment for herself and those around her. Like the meetings, smoking breaks on the company balcony were opportunities to bitch about unfairness and the corporate hierarchy to anyone within earshot. If only we would all listen to her, she would put everything right. But nobody ever did, so what was the point of her even trying?

Needless to say, Teresa's toxic attitude dampened meetings, stalled brainstorming, and caused meeting organizers to leave her out of the mix even when her input would have been valuable to the process. (And consequently, processes that were developed in such meetings would sometimes be faulty and would require Teresa's expertise to fix them. No wonder she thought no one listened to her!)

What she wanted most of all was a promotion. If she could be a supervisor, then people would have to listen to her. People would do things correctly under her supervision. She would get a raise and share in the wealth that she imagined the company officers were hoarding unfairly. All of her years of experience, technical expertise, and fixing broken things would finally be recognized and acknowledged.

How likely was that to happen? Not in a million years.

When Teresa's group finally came under my supervision, she had been with the company for many more years than I had. Because I was well liked by the staff and had a reputation for listening, her cries for attention became louder and louder. She thought

I might actually be able to hear her, recognize her strengths, and then give her the promotion she felt she so richly deserved. And I did hear her. I just didn't agree with what she was yelling.

It all came to a head one afternoon when I asked her to come into my office to talk to her immediate supervisor and me. I explained that I understood her desire to be promoted to supervisor level. And that it was never going to happen.

The next part wasn't pretty. She cried. She screamed. She banged her fist on the wall. After I pointed out how toxic she'd become to herself and others, she grew calm. I told her that if our company created that much anger inside her, she should consider leaving, because it just wasn't healthy. For *her*. Alternatively, she needed to figure out how to re-create her relationship with the company and the people she worked with so that it was mutually nurturing.

Not too long after this conversation, I was promoted to another division, and Teresa's supervisor no longer reported to me. I don't know how Teresa coped after that, but I do know that sometime later I ran into her coming down the escalators. She gave me a smile. I said, "How's it going, Teresa?" She replied, "Great! I just got laid off." Her layoff came with a severance package, and she couldn't have been happier. Finally, Teresa would be able to get out of the "horrible" place she'd worked in for almost thirty years.

What went wrong with Teresa's career? Her belief system had become a dark and tangled web in which she got herself stuck.

In your own life, is it possible that you have beliefs that say you're not good enough to get promoted, or that you're better at your job than your coworkers, or that your boss has it in for you, or that you're just there to serve? If you're a business owner, you might believe that no one would give you capital, or that you're stuck with your business model, or that your service is exemplary.

What do you really believe about this part of you, the professional part of you? What do you believe about your capabilities and value? What do you believe are your strengths and weaknesses? What do you believe about your coworkers, the market, your company, and your chances? Do your beliefs serve you, or are they holding you back?

To help you get a handle on this area of your belief management system, I've brought some decoherence concepts to the table — possibility agility and probability fragility. In the following exercise, these will better align your beliefs with your vision. After that, you can use the belief creation tool that we first explored in chapter 6 to stabilize the new beliefs that will support the creation of your dream career.

MY CAREER ALIGNMENT WORKSHEET

BELIEF ALIGNMENT

When we feel challenged, we are usually carrying around a collection of "evidence" that does not serve us. In this exercise, write down in the "Probability Fragility" column some of the evidence that threatens your vision. Then, in the "Possibility Agility" column, counter that evidence with some disconfirming evidence that supports the fact that you can break out of the confines of your beliefs about the present. I've given you some examples to get you started.

PROBABILITY FRAGILITY	POSSIBILITY AGILITY
I'll never get promoted.	I've already been promoted once.
I have no idea how to get funding.	I will find a mentor to help me.
I don't have the skills to change careers.	I can learn new skills.

PROBABILITY FRAGILITY

_____

_____

_____

_____

_____

POSSIBILITY AGILITY

_____

_____

_____

_____

_____

ACTION ALIGNMENT

In this exercise, list actions that are part of your regular repertoire, but that won't support your vision. Then list new actions
that you will use to disrupt the ones that aren't working for you.
I've given you an example here too.

I DON'T SUPPORT MY VISION WHEN I . . . argue with my coworkers, because
it detracts from my productivity,

SO INSTEAD I WILL . . . have a calm conversation and/or refuse to participate in inflammatory conversations.

I DON'T SUPPORT MY VISION WHEN I . . . _____

_____ ,

SO INSTEAD I WILL . . . _____

_____ .

I DON'T SUPPORT MY VISION WHEN I . . . _____

_____ ,

SO INSTEAD I WILL . . . _____

_____ .

I DON'T SUPPORT MY VISION WHEN I . . . _____

_____ ,

SO INSTEAD I WILL . . . _____

_____ .

I DON'T SUPPORT MY VISION WHEN I . . . _____

_____ ,

SO INSTEAD I WILL . . . _____

_____ .

You spent many years constructing the beliefs that got you where you are today in your career or business. Some of them are serving you, and some are holding you back. You can amplify the power of your current positive beliefs about yourself and your situation by creating new supporting or dominant beliefs to go along with them and then practicing those beliefs using the following tools.

MY BELIEF CREATION PLAN TO SUPPORT MY CHOSEN PURSUIT

Belief Creation Tools

(For suggestions on using these tools, refer to chapter 3.)

MEDITATION. Quiet your mind by focusing on a phrase, an object, your breath, or the guidance of another, in order to enhance self-awareness.

A PRACTICE OF CONTEMPLATION AND REFLECTION. Use this regular, dedicated time alone to focus on, amplify, and embed particular thoughts and ideas crucial to creating your dream.

VISUALIZATION. Picture in your mind's eye a situation as you dream it can be.

IMMERSIVE PROBLEM SOLVING. Engage in the "doing" of the belief that is being created in order to absorb the belief. (For example, if your new belief is that career success comes to you easily, how would you apply this belief in real-world situations?)

THE IMAGINED AUDIENCE. Pretend to relate the story of your success in a public forum, whether you imagine a single confidante or a large group.

BLOGGING. Share the creation of your dream by posting online at least daily using free or paid blogging tools on the Internet to create a public journal of your success.

VLOGGING. Use a video camera to record each post, as opposed to text. Can also be used in combination with blogging.

JOURNALING. Create a "success journal" to capture the qualities of your dream life in writing, and update it at least weekly.

PRAYER. Communicate with the deity of your choice, according to the religious tradition of your choice, to make requests regarding the creation of your dream life and to extend gratitude.

PRE-THANKING. Thank the Powers That Be as if your dream creation has already come true. (Which it has; we're just waiting for it to show up here.)

Do you have some belief creation tools that you are already using with great success? Record them here and use them everywhere in the creation process.

CUSTOM BELIEF CREATION TOOL #1 _____

_____

CUSTOM BELIEF CREATION TOOL #2 _____

_____

CUSTOM BELIEF CREATION TOOL #3 _____

_____

Your Belief Creation Commitment

Choose no more than five belief creation tools from the list above, and use them to create a powerful state of belief about the creation of your dream life. Set a schedule for using them and commit to it.

TOOL	M	T	W	TH	F	S	SU
JOURNALING			X			X	

DECOHERE IT

Whether your work environment is a studio, a corner office, a home office, or a cubicle, it's part of the universal environment that's ready and willing to help you turn your dream career into reality. To leverage that universal environment, present it with a robust and stable vision of your dream career, and take action to create as much information about your dream career as you possibly can.

The first step is to create an informational record in the universal environment by writing an action plan to bring your dream career to life. It doesn't have to be anything fancy, but it should probably include the following elements:

1. **RESEARCH.** What do you need in order to amplify your dream career into reality? An understanding of job requirements, a written business plan, an answer to a problem that's been plaguing the business, or funding? Write down what you need to find out.

2. **EDUCATION.** Do you need a different degree, sales training, or a better understanding of financial documents? Are any certifications required?

3. **NETWORKING.** Who in your network can help you turn your dream career into reality? Who can provide you with a recommendation letter, an endorsement, a connection, or a resource?

4. **TIME LINE.** When will your creation be complete? Decide when you will complete each step of your creation process — and make it measurable!

5. **EXPERIENCE.** Do you need experience performing a particular task or skill critical to your chosen pursuit? How can you get it?

The second step is to publicize your intention, what I like to call creating "verbal information records" in the environment. Tell your story. Depending on the politics surrounding your choice, you may choose to share your dream with just a few close friends and business associates or everybody you know. If your goal is to get promoted, letting your boss in on it is not a bad idea. If you intend to grow your business rapidly and then sell it, informing your employees that there are new goals will definitely help. The idea is to get your vision out into the world and shared with others who can facilitate your creation process. The more succinctly you're able to state what you intend to create, the more likely you will draw to yourself the resources and opportunities that are perfectly matched with your vision.

The third step is to start taking action, the most tangible way to create information in the environment that says you intend to bring your vision to life. Taking control of your own professional growth and education is a powerful action. Reach out beyond your job description and explore. Join an industry association. Take a class. Spend time reading industry journals. More important, read journals that will expose you to ideas happening in other industries to broaden your knowledge base. Call at least three people who have the career you desire and ask them how they got there or how they create success every day. Look for potential partners: join forces with people or organizations with similar goals, and find ways you can mutually benefit. Ask for help. Offer help. Rewrite your resume. Do some market research. Prepare a successor to replace you when you move on. Your calling will have its own special action earmarks. Do at least one thing every day that tells the universe your vision is powerful and robust and will come true.

The fourth step is to spend time concentrating on your vision, visualizing your desired outcome. We all have a tendency to get wrapped up in the logistical stuff from day to day. It's critical to spend time resisting what needs to be done in order to *design* what needs to be done. The best strategizing happens in those moments when you give yourself permission to spend time thinking about and perfecting your vision.

If you feel as if some of your current actions or ways of being in the world prevent you from bringing your dream career to life, you might go back to chapter 6 and do the "Possibility Agility" exercise as it relates to your chosen pursuit.

APPLY THE INVERSE ZENO EFFECT

Eight months after I'd been hired to manage the internal computer support department of the *Miami Herald*, I was asked to take on the management of a large-scale, cross-divisional project that would require almost a year to complete. My job was to make sure that each division adequately defined its own role in the project and met not only a time line that worked for them but also the overarching project time line. To do this, I used a combination of semimonthly meetings and a software program called Microsoft Project. Each division sent me a spreadsheet of the tasks they would have to accomplish, and I input all the tasks into a single project file. Each task had a deadline. The meetings were designed to determine whether all the tasks that should have been completed by that date had been, and if not, why and what could be done to get them back on track.

The process worked beautifully, for a number of reasons. First, nobody wanted to be called out in front of all the other divisions for having missed a deadline, so accountability was built in. Second, using the Microsoft Project file, everyone was able to determine the "critical path" of the project — that is, which activities could make or break the time line of the whole program, providing focus where it was needed most. Third, our discussions provided us with the opportunity to regularly examine our process and figure out if we still felt we were taking the best approach. The Microsoft Project file became our yardstick. It was the system by which we measured our performance and the successful execution of our project.

When planning a change in your career, you too will need the equivalent of a Microsoft Project file: a master plan against which you can measure your progress. This written master plan is a tool to help you be accountable to yourself and will direct your focus where it's needed most. Your regular review of the plan will allow you to reexamine your objectives and direction to see if you're still on the right track, or to determine whether the track should be moved. When developing this master action plan, consider this: what key measurements will drive your daily activity and accelerate the arrival of your dream career?

If you want to be an author, for example, you might set daily writing goals for yourself. You can then measure your effort to achieve those goals, and if you can't meet them, you can develop a contingency plan to get there. On the other hand, you might decide that a daily goal doesn't work for your lifestyle, and that a weekly goal might be better.

If you want to get a promotion, you might decide that growing and maintaining your organizational network is critical. You might choose a measurement that says you'll add two people to your network every week, or that you will solidify your network by providing at least two members with something of value each week.

If you want to grow your business, you will no doubt need to set sales and marketing goals. Increasing your company's sales by a certain percentage every month is a great place to start. Setting the number of prospects that must be called on to achieve those goals is another key metric. You might also decide to focus on increasing the number of transactions per customer per month by a specific number, or on increasing the size of each of those transactions.

Remember, the purpose of these measurements is to bolster your confidence and guide you gently toward your objective, not punish yourself. Here's a tool I like to use to help me stay on track: the Inverse Zeno Report, or IZR. It's simple. Every day, keep a list of all the things you did that were productive, particularly those activities linked to the realization of your vision. You can use a simple piece of paper for this or record it in your day planner. I like to use an email message. I record everything I accomplish during the day as I go, taking positive measurements of my progress. When I first started using this tool, at the end of the day I would send it to my then-fiancé, Michael. He would write back, saying something like, "Way to go! You're amazing, honey!" Or: "You're slaying dragons today! Great job!" You too might want to send your report to someone who supports you, whether that's your significant other, your mom, or your accountability partner. That extra pat on the back doesn't hurt!

Over time, as I have used this tool, its value and purpose have significantly changed. At first I wrote the IZR to make me feel better, to reinforce the idea that I was actually getting important things done during the day. Later, I began to list in advance the things I wanted to accomplish, with a space separating them from the things I'd already done, so that it became a sort of to-do list. As I finished something, I moved it from the bottom list to the top list.

Now, just so you know, I've kept to-do lists for most of my life, and I manage my tasks daily in Microsoft Entourage, but somehow, the IZR list became more important. In it I recorded my real top priorities on any given day. It told me what I needed to get done to walk away from my desk each night and feel really good about my creation process. The IZR metamorphosed from a report of past activity to a predictor and director of future activity. I wanted to take more positive measurements of myself.

These days, I'm so focused on my creation process that I don't need to file an IZR with my significant other. But if I have a bad day, all those sent emails are right there in one place, and I can look back at them and remember how incredibly powerful I am as a creator.

Give the Inverse Zeno Report a try this week, and see how taking positive measurements of yourself throughout the day makes you feel about yourself and influences the way you act.

8. AMP UP YOUR LOVE LIFE
AND RELATIONSHIPS

Intensifying Your Connections

I WAS MARRIED FOR NINE YEARS. After the divorce was final, I spent the next twelve years amplifying a series of relationship possibilities for all the wrong reasons. First, I tried more than once to re-create what I'd just given up (despite the fact that it had made me so unhappy that I'd felt compelled to end it). When that didn't work, I realized I needed to get clear about what I wanted and write down my vision.

Reviewing my vision statement later, I was astonished to discover that I'd written an antivision: "Give me a relationship that is not my past marriage!" Well, I'd gotten half of it written down, at least. But here was the issue: the kind of relationship I wanted wouldn't come to me if all I could envision was the antimatter and not the matter.

I rewrote the vision. The men came and went. Quickly. It was rare that I went out on a second date with anyone. This gave me pause. I worried that I was being too judgmental, that I wasn't giving these guys a chance. So I went out on a few second and third dates. Nope. I was right. My heart knew the truth in one date.

I bought a bunch of books with titles like *Find a Husband after 35 Using What I Learned at Harvard Business School* and *Expect a Miracle: 7 Spiritual Steps to Finding the Right Relationship*, and I was beginning to think that a miracle was exactly what I needed.

I looked for available men everywhere. I examined the men I worked with, reported to, and supervised. I sought them at night-clubs, community events, and friends' barbecues. I looked for them online and hired services to find them for me. The first agency I hired went belly-up, taking my promised men with them. I received a letter from the clerk of the court informing me that as a creditor of the business, I might be entitled to some portion of the bankruptcy proceeds. To claim it, I needed to write a letter. So I did.

Dear Clerk:

I am submitting copies of my Visa credit card statements along with this narrative as proof of payments made to Together of Miami for matchmaking services purchased and never rendered.

Tallahassee Intro, Inc., a.k.a. Together of Miami, fulfilled one-half of its contractual obligation, having introduced me to only six men rather than twelve, none of which proved satisfactory. Since I paid my contract in full in 1995 in two payments, $1,000 and $850, I believe that the debtor still owes me $925, or six men.

Tallahassee Intro, Inc., can repay this debt in dollars or in men, whichever it has more readily at hand.

I eagerly await the determination of the court in this matter.

Very truly yours, . . .

At least I had a sense of humor about it.

In fact, I had a cocktail party joke about the men in my hometown of Miami. Holding my hands about shoulder width apart, I'd say, "Here are all the men in Miami." I'd move my hands closer together. "Here are all the straight men." I'd move them even closer. "Here are the available men." Closer. "Here are the well-adjusted men." Closer still. "Here are the intelligent" — closer — "good-looking" — closer — "athletic men, and you can see what my opportunities are!" By this time, my palms were, of course, pressed firmly together, without room for even an air molecule, much less a man.

Gee. Could the trouble have been me?

I went back and rewrote my vision. Over the course of that twelve years, I had a couple of relationships — three years here, one year there — but mostly just dates and, finally, in the last few years, not much of anything. On the bad days, I worried that I would end up alone, a spinster. On the good days, I relished the control I had over my own life plan, the weekend mornings with which I could do whatever I wanted, and the way I could splay myself over the entire mattress of my king-sized bed without kicking anybody.

Eventually, I decided that it would be perfectly okay if I stayed single for the rest of my life. I had a good life: plenty of friends, a lot of social functions to attend, a great son, a wonderful family, and engaging work. I decided I didn't *need* a love relationship in order to be happy, that my life was full and satisfying enough, and that there was a lot more where that came from. I had finally applied one of the fundamental tools for opening up to possibility: I had accepted the worst possible outcome as far as a love relationship: I might never have one.

Further, I decided that if my man were out there, he and I would meet eventually. So I left it up to the universe and stopped trying to make it happen.

That's when Michael showed up. Michael and I had both signed up to be mentors for an industry fellowship program. We met each other for the first time at the fellowship kickoff meeting in Orlando. Nothing more than a smile and a nod passed between us, as there was a series of speakers and not much time between presentations for chatting. Then I bolted off to spend time with my family, who lives near there.

Our second meeting took place in Shakopee Valley, Minnesota, a bedroom community of Minneapolis, where the fellowship's client newspaper was located. Michael and I spent three days together there, got to know each other much better, and had a lot of fun. After that interlude, he started sending me emails from his home base of Augusta, Georgia — emails full of poetry and romance. I answered them from Miami. We graduated to nightly phone calls. Finally, we agreed that we needed to see each other again in person and decide if this relationship could really go anywhere.

We've been together ever since. We both feel as if we've just begun to discover the possibilities our relationship will offer us. We feel very blessed. So, why, we both wondered, hadn't we met each other sooner?

Recently I went back and spent some time with my vision again. Here's what I discovered. My vision wasn't big enough. I hadn't even remotely amped it up. I had written a safe vision, a not-too-ambitious vision: a vision of love and respect, certainly, but nothing out of the ordinary. It was not a vision of big love, of magnificent love. I was not looking for someone who could take my idea of love to the next level.

Thinking about it now, it's evident that part of the reason was that I was afraid of that kind of commitment. If my partner had high expectations about my participation in the relationship... what if I couldn't come through? What if I wasn't good enough?

What if I couldn't engage as deeply as my partner? Before I even began, I was afraid of failing.

It is also clear to me now that in my youth I wasn't inner-directed when choosing men. Rather, I went with the flow, allowing men to choose me and relationships to just appear in my life, instead of seeking out the kind of man and kind of relationship I wanted. But how could I pursue the relationship I wanted when I hadn't even defined it in my own heart? As Yogi Berra said, "If you don't know where you are going, you might wind up someplace else." Wind up someplace else I did.

Michael knew what he wanted when he met me. He wanted a big love. He wanted to treasure and be treasured. After many years in a passionless marriage, he was no longer willing to settle for less. He wanted a vibrant love that would resonate in his soul, require care and attention, and nurture him in spiritual ways. Through Michael's vision, I was able to start addressing my fears and open my heart. Through his vision, I began to amp up my own vision of what an ideal relationship could be.

Another discovery I made in reviewing my vision was that I was looking for a man to fulfill the role of stepfather to my son Zack. I needed someone to love him and be there for him, and I stopped dating a couple of men because of the way they interacted with my son, the way I thought they would interact with my son, or because they didn't want to interact with my son. I was almost more concerned about Zack being happy with the man I chose than with my own happiness with that man. You can imagine that making a choice like that would not serve Zack or me in the long run. It seems perfect, then, that in addition to Michael being a great match for me, he's also pitch perfect with my son.

Lastly, I figured out that I had been asking myself the wrong questions, and so had limited the possibilities available to me. Luckily, along the way I sought out and encountered guides able to suggest a different focus for my questioning, and over time I reframed my questions to get to the heart of my desires.

This experience taught me that it's entirely possible to stymie your creation process with fear, unexamined beliefs, and the desire for instantaneous gratification in your life, rather than to seek out and create something much bigger, beautiful, and new. You may be applying all the steps of the amplification process but generating unintentional results because your vision is crippled, still just a shadow of what it could be, or missing key components that aren't clear to you now.

If you aren't firing on all pistons in a particular area of your life, and you really want to be, go back and look at the motives behind your vision. Are you prioritizing security or growth? Are you seeking to prevent a recurrence of bad things that happened in the past, or are you forging a new and brighter path for the future? Are you prioritizing your own desires or what others think of you or wish for you?

Sometimes the hardest part of creating a powerful vision is getting to our own clear desires. That's why so many books have been published about finding your passion or purpose in life. If you haven't yet taken the journey to the place in your own heart where your truest dreams lie, delay no longer. Pack a lunch and get on the road.

THE DEFINITION OF *RELATIONSHIP*

Although I've spent several pages talking specifically about romantic love and committed relationships, you can apply the Possibility Amplification Process to any relationship in your life, whether that relationship is with your parents, your children, your friends, or your coworkers. I am a witness to the fact that the richness and vibrancy of relationships can be amplified. Even the most difficult relationships can be reframed to open up possibilities you never knew existed in them.

Because relationships are based on emotional attachments, yours may challenge you more than any other part of your life. On the other hand, everyone has different strengths. You could be a master at relationships — even if you're in total consternation over how to manage your finances, for example. Whether you consider yourself a relationship master, a relationship rookie, or something in between, you can use the possibility amplification techniques that the universe uses and create even more satisfying and rewarding relationships.

If you're wondering whether amping up your relationships is worth your time, energy, and prioritization, let me tell you a story. My mother was eighteen and pregnant with me when her mother, Gwendolyn, died suddenly from a brain aneurysm. My mother's parents lived in a suburb of Chicago. My father was in the military, and he and my mother were stationed in Georgia. Although they raced to get there, my grandmother was gone before my mother could reach her side.

At the time of my grandmother's death, she and my mother were not exactly getting along well. My mother's rebellious adolescence and her mother's inability to understand her daughter's choices had heavily taxed the relationship. Consequently, my mom was left with all the things she wished she could have said to and done for her mother. It took her years to work out her feelings about the way things were between them when her mother died.

At eighteen, it is highly unlikely that my mother realized the true value of her relationship with her mother. Most teenagers don't. Only in her mother's absence, and with maturity, did the value of the relationship become evident. Even those of us who are much older and supposedly wiser often take our relationships for granted until a friendship is broken or a child no longer visits, until divorce papers are served or death robs us of a loved one unexpectedly and too soon.

But it doesn't have to be that way for you. The universe's ability to deliver unlimited possibility means that you can have it all: money, a great career, fame, adventure, and whatever you have wished for, including fabulous relationships.

Along the way and in the end, our loved ones surround us in our times of need. The relationships we have cultivated and nurtured are a tangible asset, one that we can count on, fall back on, and use to lift us up. Your investment in this asset will give you much better returns than what you're getting in the stock market, guaranteed.

ACCESSING THE POSSIBILITIES

Have you fully crafted the vision of your dream relationship? You may have a particular relationship in mind. If you're single and looking for a great love relationship, or currently in a friendship or love relationship you'd like to improve, or wishing you could be more comfortable with your parents or children, or would like to get along better with a coworker, then getting clear on what you want your relationship to look like will propel you in the right direction. Take a moment and get yourself in wave mode to open up to the possibilities. You can use the questions in the following sections to do this.

What Does a Successful Relationship Look Like to You?

How challenging is it? Does it encourage you to grow or to accept yourself just the way you are? How does the relationship make you feel about yourself? Is it warm and fuzzy, or would it be great if it just weren't toxic? Does it feel intimate? Is there mutual respect? How balanced is the attention in the relationship? How much attention do you need? How authentic can you be? Does

your significant other or friend or family member respect your secrets, or do you share everything? What tone does the relationship
have? Is it upbeat? A bitchfest? Laid back? Do you have warm
camaraderie? What kind of behavior is acceptable? What's not?
If this relationship were the way you envision it, what would it
look like?

Let's talk about your life vision in the context of a love relationship first. Perhaps in your dream relationship, you and your
mate love doing the same things. Maybe you love introducing each
other to new experiences and ideas. Perhaps you shower each
other with material gifts. Or you value physical affection more
than things. Will you provide each other with personal services,
such as the needed neck rub or icy cold cocktail, without even
being asked?

How will you reinforce your love and your bond? Will you
have a special way to communicate with your loved one? Will it
be a priority for you to remind each other regularly of your love
for one another?

In your dream relationship, you and your mate could find fun
and novel ways to tell each other how you feel. In a recent issue
of a women's magazine, I read a story about a couple who told
each other "I love you" by making some kind of contact three
times in a row, one time for each of the words in "I love you."
Sometimes it was three squeezes of the hand. Three pats on the
shoulder. Three eyeblinks from across the table.

Another couple made up acronyms for their shared common
expressions, so with just a few letters and in perfect privacy they
could tell each other what they thought about the event they were
attending, or their hostess's dress, or each other.

What promises will you make to each other? Will you always
kiss each other good night? Never go to bed angry? Never tear
each other down in front of the kids?

If the relationship you would like to amplify is other than your love relationship, what would that relationship look like if it were successful? Perhaps you would seek more detachment from the other person's thoughts and deeds. For example, the other person would still say and do the same things, but you wouldn't have the strong emotional reaction you do now. Or maybe she'd say the same things, but you'd love her anyway.

You might desire an authentic relationship in which you can be perfectly yourself and be accepted and cherished for who you are. You might also wish to be brave enough to say exactly what's on your mind, even though you know the other person won't like it. Respect for your time and resources, regular times to get together, and variety in your mutual activities or conversational topics are all desirable possibilities. Of course, you might like these kinds of characteristics in a love relationship as well.

Put a Time Frame on Starting Your Perfect Relationship

If you would like to improve your relationship with your mother, when would you like to feel more peace in your relationship with her? When would you like to forgive her? When would you like to see her weaknesses as just that, rather than as a statement about who you are?

If your vision includes beginning a love relationship, by what date would you like to have a special person appear in your life? The great thing about setting milestones is that even when you're not consciously thinking about them, your mind is still working on making them happen. A focus is created by an intention that helps you see and take advantage of opportunities that you might otherwise not notice. As the date approaches, your mind is looking for your new lover to appear or for your conflict with a loved one to turn the corner. You might accept an invitation to a party, for

CAUTION

Let me throw out a caution here. Just because you have a specific vision of how you would like to conduct your relationship with someone else, this is no guarantee that the other person feels the same way. Remember, each of us is a creator, and your relationship partner may be amplifying a personal vision that has nothing to do with your desires. Your partner may not even be aware that he or she is amplifying anything at all.

If it turns out that your visions are quite different... what's your contingency plan? Some people choose distance to solve that problem, and that may be the best solution available for some relationships. Other relationships might need to be ended if the visions are too disparate. You may continue to invest in a relationship because of its importance to you, even if that means you and your partner are mutually amplifying a compromise vision. In that case, what is the best possible outcome you can imagine that would serve both visions?

Now let me throw out caution #2: don't envision a contingency dream before envisioning your primary dream. First describe in detail what you would like to have happen. Keep your vision as pure as possible. You want to start your creation process from the best possible place, not from a compromised position.

example, even though you're tired and normally wouldn't go. Or all of a sudden you might find one of your friend's annoying comments amusing instead. Choosing a time limit by which you expect change to take place reinforces the depth of your intention to create your desired outcome.

Revel in the Feelings You Will Have

When your relationship vision comes true, will you feel excitement? Blissful joy? Peace and contentment? Gratification or relief? Will you go to bed with a smile on your lips and wake up with it still there? Decide that you will experience the emotions of your new relationship starting now. Begin to practice those feelings and bring them into your life. By doing so, you may find yourself attracting just the sort of relationship response you've been looking for.

Inspire Your Visioning Process with the Stories of Others

Almost everyone you know has a story about how he or she fixed a friendship, rekindled a romance, met the person of his or her dreams, or smoothed things out with a child or parent. One of my favorite books of stories about love relationships is *Project Everlasting: Two Bachelors Discover the Secrets of America's Greatest Marriages* by Mathew Boggs and Jason Miller. If you're disenchanted with love, this book will reenchant you. The couples interviewed for the book are absolutely charming, and the love-bumbling bachelor authors reveal some of the typical fears and concerns we've all had at one time or another when it comes to love. The book may inspire you to add some features to your relationship vision that may not have occurred to you.

Does your family or circle of friends have any great love stories or reconciliation stories? Does your religion or spiritual practice offer a guide to great relationships?

What does history reveal about the greatest loves of all time? Would you, like Napoleon, ask your wife not to bathe until you arrive home — in three days — just so you could smell her pure essence? Would you, like Josephine Bonaparte, do it gladly? Do you dream of building a Taj Mahal to honor your most supreme lover, as Shah Jahan, ruler of the Mughal empire, did? Would you forsake everything, including your honor, to be with your love, as Antony did for Cleopatra? Do you hope you'll get asked to? Do you hope you'll find *the one* who could make you want to?

Ahhh, love! With these sorts of questions, we're beginning to...

AMP IT UP!

Now that you've put some ideas on paper about how you would like your relationships to function, whether with family members, friends, lovers, or coworkers, let's see if we can't amp that vision up and give it more heart and substance.

Just like Dr. Seuss's Grinch in *The Grinch Who Stole Christmas*, perhaps we can imagine and then bring to life a whole different way of being with other people. As you may recall, the Grinch had a heart three sizes too small. But through his observation of the people of Whoville, he learned about and internalized the importance of relationships. In the animated version of the book, the Grinch's cartoon heart grew and grew until it burst through the X-ray device examining it, because it was so big.

I want your heart to grow and grow until you feel like you could burst with happiness because of all the rich rewards you receive from your relationships. If you want that too, then take some time for yourself and answer the questions in the following worksheet.

AMP UP YOUR RELATIONSHIPS! WORKSHEET

The first eleven questions are designed to get you thinking about all the relationships that exist in your life in addition to your romances. See if you might like to expand your vision and create a reality in which you are conscious of your connections to everyone and possibly everything. In that reality you design a way of being and interacting in the world that lets you put aside momentary emotional upset, petty behavior by others, and unexpected setbacks. In that reality, there is always someone to turn to for comfort.

1. Do you wish to become closer to your parents? What risk would you have to take for that to happen?

2. Is your relationship with your siblings everything it could be or that you want it to be?

3. What might be the benefit of reaching out to your extended family, of reconnecting with cousins, aunts, and uncles? Is there a family historian who will pass down the legacy stories to the next generations? Could you be that historian or encourage someone else to be one?

4. Do you desire a closer relationship with your children or stepchildren? If you could eliminate one barrier, what would it be?

5. Do you desire to reconnect with someone you've lost touch with? Who is that?

6. Would you like to have as tight a relationship with your in-laws as you have with your blood relatives?

7. Could you be an inspiration to your coworkers? Offer your services as a mentor? Give your coworkers more space to do their jobs?

8. Perhaps you'd like to really connect with the strangers you meet every day, by sharing a smile, looking them in the eye, or attentively listening to their answers to "How are you?"

9. Would you like to adopt a pet? Or take better care of the one you have? Do you wish you could take in a stray that no one else wants?

10. Is there a relationship with nature you'd like to have, with the Earth, with the universe?

11. Are you experiencing or would you like to experience the fullness of a relationship with God or another higher power?

When defining a vision of how your relationships could be in each of these circumstances, you might focus on just a few things, such as how you'd like to stop fighting so much, or how a specific type of relationship is missing from your life. Just fixing the problems, or getting into a relationship at all, might seem like a pretty tall order. Yet if you wish to hang on to these relationships — once you've got them — and get them to blossom, you might consider a more holistic approach to your vision, one that anticipates forward movement in fulfilling your mutual desires. Here are some questions to help you think through that for all the relationships in your life.

12. How much would you like to communicate? What kinds of things will be important for you to talk about?

13. How much time would you like to devote to this relationship? How much time would you like your relationship partner to devote? Are you concerned more about quantity or quality? How would you like each of you to prioritize time spent?

14. What roles will each of you fill in the relationship? How will you share responsibilities and privileges?

15. What kinds of services will you provide for each other? Will you lend a sympathetic ear? Provide transportation? Offer foot rubs? Care for each other's children?

16. How will you maintain your connection? With a regular date on Friday nights? Daily or weekly emails?

Visits on holidays? Nightly phone calls? Dinner together every night?

17. How much attention will be devoted to this relationship, and in what ways? Will you promise each other
to really listen? Agree to leave work at the office? Will
you leave your Blackberry at home on family vacations? Turn off the TV when the family's at dinner?

18. How much physical contact will there be in this relationship? Do you want to hug more or have sex
more? Would you like to hold hands? Get an occasional pat on the back? What other kinds of physical
contact would be meaningful for you?

Lastly, I encourage you to add one particular relationship to your
list and prioritize its development above all others. The relationship I propose is with yourself. If you have not amped up your relationship with yourself, it's doubtful that you'll be able to create
the kinds of connections with others you dream about.

To explain why, let me take you back to our discussion about
epigenetics and belief. If you have a relationship with yourself
that is less than it could be, that is perhaps more punitive than supportive, for example, then that's probably what you can expect
from your other relationships. If you have an adversarial relationship with yourself in which you mentally beat yourself up, you
will no doubt be shut down much of the time. It's very difficult to
create intimacy when you're shut down or in protective mode.
When there's so much darkness inside your own head, it's hard to
open up and be vulnerable with yourself, much less anyone else.
If you're well connected with and kind to yourself, the power
of that growth mode will serve as the basis for your other relationships. The great news is that you can start to change your

relationship with yourself today. In each moment, you can choose how you will treat yourself.

To help you create a vision of the excellent and supportive relationship you would like to have with yourself, use the following questions as thought starters.

19. How often would you like to focus on communicating with yourself?

20. How much time do you need to spend alone in order to be fully connected with yourself and keep yourself in balance?

21. What kinds of activities would help you to grow this relationship? Meditation? Physical exercise? Therapy? What kind of commitment would you like to make there?

22. How willing are you to forgive your own missteps? Can you imagine a life in which you are gentle with yourself when you make mistakes?

23. How much attention will you devote to your own care and well-being? How will you prioritize these over everything else going on in your life?

24. What kinds of gifts can you give yourself or allow yourself to have? What would be most important to you to receive? Love? Material things? Time?

25. What kind of commitment will you make to treat yourself with the love and kindness you would offer a treasured friend or beloved family member?

BELIEF MANAGEMENT

It's often easier to believe that you can amp up your financial situation more easily than your relationships, because money doesn't talk back. It doesn't slam the door, and it doesn't scream at you. Money, as an inanimate object, has no mind of its own, whereas the people in your life have beliefs and motivations that sometimes don't match your own. Given that you can't control how others think and behave, how could you create a set of beliefs concerning your ability to create fabulous relationships when perhaps the people you're engaged with don't seem to have a clue?

Here's the truth about relationships: you can control only who you want to be in those relationships. That is, you can only strive to create a foundational set of beliefs that will help you be the best possible participant you can be in your relationships, no matter what the other people in the relationships are doing.

In your existing relationships, you may be holding on to beliefs that do not serve you. For example, in a love relationship, you may believe

1. you always have to be right;
2. it's your job to keep your partner happy at all times; or
3. winning arguments is more important than nurturing the relationship (so you pursue conquest at any cost).

In your family and wider social circle you might believe

1. your dad has always thought poorly of you;
2. your mom is weak; or
3. your best friend is flawless.

Do you see the difference between the first set of beliefs and the latter set of beliefs? The first three are about you, whereas the latter three are about the people you are in relationships with. Tackling the first set of beliefs, the beliefs you have about how *you* would like to operate in relationships, is where all the gold is.

The goal of belief management is to modify your beliefs to the point where you feel you are generally acting from positive motives and for the good of both participants in the relationship. (I say "generally" because none of us is perfect, and at times we do things out of pettiness, crankiness, and other not-so-positive motivations.)

Once you are firmly grounded in your beliefs and the value of those beliefs, you will find it much easier to separate the impact of your participation on the quality of the relationship from the impact of your relationship partner's behavior. You will see where you begin and the other person ends. At that point, you can begin to separate your "stuff" from the other person's "stuff" ("stuff" being the baggage from the past that we all carry into our relationships). Even though the two of you may have packed those bags together over time, your stuff is still your own. By examining and being conscious of the beliefs driving your behavior, you can decide to carry just your own baggage and let your relationship partner carry his or hers.

How can you discover the beliefs driving your behavior in relationships? First, let me assure you that you don't have to do this process alone. If you feel that having an outside, unbiased opinion would be helpful, then do seek out the help of a psychotherapist or trained counselor who can help you identify your beliefs about relationships. I worked through a lot of my own thoughts about relationships by having a counselor as an impartial sounding board from time to time.

At one point in my past, I belonged to a divorce support group, and the women in that group really helped me learn more about my beliefs and myself. In fact, I was able to spot faulty beliefs held by the other members, only to realize later that I suffered from the same faulty beliefs! Without having that mirror to look in, I might never have discovered those particular truths about myself. Peer groups can be a good resource too.

If you intend to embark on this discovery process solo — and that's a great method too — then I have a few tips on how to start. First, let's refer back to your vision. You might have stated that you intend to create a close and loving relationship with your parents, or that you will be more emotionally available to your kids, or that you will find a new love and build a great love relationship. For the purpose of this explanation, let's take that last one — find a new love and build a great love relationship — as our example.

First, look back at the love relationships that are no longer in your life. Why are they gone? How did they end? Looking back from your perspective today, what have you learned about your beliefs from your time with those people? Did the relationships end due to faulty beliefs, faulty motives, or faulty expectations? The reasons for terminating a relationship can almost always be traced back to one of those three things.

Second, look back at the love relationships that were, at least for a time, successful. Which were the most successful? What made them successful? What do you believe about those relationships, your participation in them, and their meaning in your life? Successful relationships in your life that are *not* love relationships can also provide you with some good ideas about what will support a healthy love relationship. If you can collect and catalog the beliefs that have served you in your successful relationships, you may discover that you can apply them to create a positive and nurturing new relationship as well.

If you have no prior love relationships in your life (and you're old enough to have been romantically in love at least once in your life), what has prevented you from being in a love relationship? Do you believe you don't deserve it, or that your time has not yet come? Do you believe you'll just end up getting hurt? Are you afraid of the physical intimacy that comes with love relationships, or have you seen really bad role models that you're afraid you'll emulate? If you've really wanted love in your life, what other fears could be holding you back? Or if you've chosen not to get involved, why has that been right for you? If you've wanted to get started on the path to love but haven't been able to do so, examining your closely held beliefs about what love relationships mean in general can be an eye-opening experience. Once you know what those beliefs are, you can begin the process of discarding those that don't serve you and choosing new beliefs that support your desire.

Now let's take the example of wanting to create a better relationship with your significant other. There are many possible beliefs that may be holding you back from creating that. Let me provide some examples to jump-start your thinking on it.

- Our problems are all his/her fault.
- All our problems are my fault.
- I can never make this person happy, no matter what.
- It's my job to make this person happy.
- Relationships are naturally confrontational.
- I'm lucky this person loves me, because I'm so unlovable.
- I deserve poor treatment, because I'm worthless.
- I can't really change this relationship.
- Sex equals love.
- My partner never listens, so there's no point in talking.
- I never win in this relationship.
- I'd rather win than be happy.
- If I apologize, it means I lose.
- He/she should spend every night with me.
- With my help, he/she will finally become the person I want him/her to be.

- Disagreement is destructive, it will rip us apart.
- If this person knew who I really was, he/she wouldn't love me anymore.
- I'll never be able to forgive what he/she did.

If you were to take the inverse of each of the beliefs just listed, you'd have a pretty good set of positive beliefs that would serve you well in your quest to improve your relationship with your significant other:

- We both have responsibility for our problems.
- Rather than seek to place blame, I focus on constructive solutions.
- Each of us has the job of treating the other person well.
- We each must be responsible for our own happiness.
- I can tolerate some confrontation in my relationships to make them better.
- I'm lucky this person loves me, and that I love him/her back.
- I am worthy, lovable, and deserve to be treated well.
- I can change this relationship by changing my participation in it.
- Love equals love. Sex equals sex. They are not substitutes for each other.
- Authentic communication is important to the health of my relationships.
- I am more interested in a strong relationship than in winning.
- When I've done something wrong, I can give the gift of apology.
- Having our own interests makes our relationship richer.
- I accept my relationship partner completely and wholly.
- Disagreeing from time to time is natural and healthy.

- I want the other person to know me as I really am.
- Forgiveness is a tool with which I heal myself.

Doesn't the second list make you feel a lot better than the first? It does me. Does either list remind you of some other beliefs that might also be holding you back, or that are positive influences? Hang on to those positive ones! They're a great foundation upon which to start building the new, magnificent love relationship of your dreams.

When you have a written collection of beliefs about each of the relationships you wish to focus on, relationships that will nurture and sustain both you and your relationship partner, you can begin to exercise those beliefs in real life by applying the techniques of decoherence.

DECOHERE IT

Decoherence planning and execution for relationships can be, in turn, painful, difficult, scary, and delightful. This is where you test out your vision, and the beliefs you've chosen to support it, on the other person in your relationship and see how he or she reacts.

You may find that your spouse, relative, coworker, friend, or child is excited about your vision and participates eagerly in order to bring it to life. Remember, though, that just because you've decided how a particular relationship should look and feel, this doesn't necessarily mean that your partner has the same vision. Your partner might like things just the way they are, in which case it will be very difficult for you to bring your vision to life *with that person.*

You may ultimately be able to amplify one part of your vision but not another. For example, you might successfully implement the part of your romantic relationship vision that says, from now on, you and your spouse won't go to bed mad at each other, but you may not be able to get your mate to play board games on weekend nights in front of the fire. At the office, you might get a coworker to stop handing you unfinished reports, but she still may show up late for your meetings.

You may make no headway at all. If you confront a parent who regularly criticizes you by telling him that the criticism is hurtful and you'd like it to stop, he may say yes or no. If your parent says he doesn't see a problem, you will then be faced with some choices. You could establish a personal policy regarding how you will respond to future criticism from him. For example, you might reply, "Thank you, I appreciate your concern," and move on to other topics. You might also decide that to preserve your own peace and inner calm, you'll no longer emotionally respond to that parent's criticism. By choosing this course of action, you could potentially receive the benefit of less criticism because your parent can't get a rise out of you anymore.

You could also decide that you'll reduce the amount of time you spend with that parent, or, depending on how abusive the relationship is, stop spending any time with that parent at all. Only you can decide how much you are willing to modify your vision of the ideal relationship in order to maintain the relationship.

Trying out new behaviors and requests in an existing relationship can feel strange, particularly in a long-standing relationship. I can guarantee moments of surprise: a request that you thought would be difficult for your partner goes over very easily, or one that you thought would be easy turns out to be complicated.

As I noted earlier, when you start changing in a relationship, you will often get "change back" messages from the person you're in the relationship with. That's okay. If you strongly believe in your vision, persevere! Eventually, you'll receive the signals that tell you whether or not your chosen possibilities are the strongest and most robust ones.

To strengthen the relationship possibilities you want to bring to life, let's focus on three main situations:

1. You want to create a relationship that does not yet exist for you.
2. You have a troubled relationship that you want to make better.
3. You have a good relationship that you want to amp up.

In the first situation, let's say that it's a love relationship you want to create. What steps can you take to communicate your desire to the environment in order to get its help turning your desire into reality? A friend and business associate of mine, widowed some years ago, used a business networking event to tell every woman in the room that she wanted to meet someone. Gutsy, and also a great use of grid amplification. A web producer friend of mine met her husband through the online dating site Match.com. Two vice presidents in an executive team I was a member of were married to each other recently. I met my former husband while camping in Key Largo with friends. I dated a man who sang along with me in the church choir. A woman who sits on the same board as I do introduced me to one of her friends. And finally, I met Michael by volunteering as a mentor in an industry association fellowship program.

You've got to get out there! If you're interested in dating Dr. McDreamy on *Grey's Anatomy* or the pizza deliveryman, then stay home and watch TV every night. But if you'd like to explore the relationship options available to you, leap into your environment with both feet. Volunteer your time, study the newspaper for events you can go to, and put a profile up on an online dating service. When I first joined Facebook, a social networking site, a friend I hadn't heard from in fifteen years sent me a note almost immediately. In this very connected day and age, it's possible to meet people whose paths you would never have crossed in your everyday life.

According to a 2008 University of Rochester study, if you're seeking to make a not-so-good relationship better, or seeking to make a good relationship outstanding, there's one decoherence technique — and a particular way of conducting your use of that technique — that will serve you well. Pro-relationship behaviors (PRBs), defined as "any sacrifice or accommodation made out of consideration for one's partner or one's relationship,"[1] have a positive impact on the quality of relationships. So if you make a point of proactively doing the dishes after dinner — or do something bigger, like agreeing to move across the country so that your partner can take a better job — it will improve your relationship.

Here's a secret that one coauthor of the study, Heather Patrick, uncovered with her research: the PRBs will have much more impact if you make sacrifices or contributions because you really want to, rather than out of obligation or in response to pressure. People who feel that their partners engage in PRBs willingly are more satisfied with and committed to their relationships. Further, by engaging in PRBs, you might inspire your partner to do the same for you, which would really amp up your relationship, wouldn't it?

PRBs are one way to put information into the environment about your intention to achieve your vision of a better relationship. Some other techniques include creating with your partner a list of the top priorities of the relationship, or of the relationship values to which you both subscribe. You could become more conscious about complimenting your relationship partner in public or showing him or her affection. You could also plan surprises, like cooking a favorite meal or inviting your partner to an event that is less to your taste and more to your partner's liking.

As I like to say, love is an action verb. You can make your love and respect tangible things in the environmental context of your relationship by performing loving acts.

MEASURING LOVE

Are you in a "tit for tat" relationship? Say you give your partner a back massage and then wait patiently and possibly forever to get one in return. Does your patience turn into impatience and then finally anger when it becomes apparent that no reciprocal back rub is in the works? You could ask for the back rub, but then the other person would just be doing it because you asked for it, not because there is loving motivation there. By being so focused on receiving gratification *in kind*, you might have missed the fact that your spouse threw away the yucky soap slivers and placed a fresh bar of soap for you in the shower, or took the kids to school when it was your turn, or folded the laundry, or maybe all three.

Relationships often go awry when one or both partners focus on the wrong measurements. The first question to ask yourself is whether you are jointly focused on measuring outcomes rather than outputs. Remember, an outcome is the end result or condition you want to create — for example, "happy marriage" — whereas outputs are the things that are delivered at the end of a process, such as "number of back rubs." If the relationship overall is healthy, respectful, and loving, but it experiences the occasional process burp, you're probably on the right track. Downplaying the focus on outputs and dialing up the focus on the desired outcome will likely help you achieve the latter.

Second, in what context are you taking these measurements? The underpinnings of some relationships, including your own, might surprise you. Often they're based on the distribution of power. If you're in a relationship in which one person is more self-focused and feels the need to be dominant, the other person may feel the need to constantly reestablish his or her autonomy. If you're in a relationship in which one partner feels comfortable subordinating himself or herself to the other, the other might feel the need to establish distance, by encouraging outside interests, for example. If both you and your partner believe in equally distributing the power in the relationship, then you will most likely settle into a state of mutuality, which recent studies say produces the healthiest outcomes.[2]

If you're measuring in a context of unequal power distribution that irritates either partner, it may be difficult to measure effectively. You and your partner will have trouble agreeing on what the right measurements are. For example, if you're a woman whose husband has proudly proclaimed himself a "dinosaur" whose picture-perfect relationship has him in the corner office and you taking care of the home and children, then your career will always be a thorn in his side. If instead your world revolves around his every move, then his late nights out with the boys and weekend golfing sessions will be the pain point. In unbalanced relationships like these, can you see how conflicting visions will always have both partners measuring success by separate and completely different systems?

For some couples, however, the unequal power distribution works well for both participants, because each person's relationship style supports it. What kind of context is provided by the power distribution in your relationship?

Relationships can also go on far longer than they should because one or both of the partners are not measuring the right things. This has a more benign form, for example, in which you don't fire the inadequately performing assistant because you keep getting great feedback about her from your customers. Or you don't quit a job that's going nowhere because you're measuring yourself more aggressively against the yardstick "loyalty" than you are against the yardstick "career success." Your relief when the assistant quits, or you do, is a good indicator that you've been measuring the wrong thing.

There is a more malignant form of measurement dysfunction

in relationships, however, in which destructive behaviors are glossed over, forgiven, or discounted, only to reappear over and over again, to the detriment of one of the partners. Destructive behaviors can include verbal abuse (hypercriticalness and condescension), overpossessiveness, substance abuse, sexual abuse, or physical abuse. If you are enduring any of these behaviors in your relationship, I urge you to seriously consider what benefit you're getting from the relationship. No amount of measurement can fix a broken spirit, the loss of your self-respect, or daily unhappiness. Stand up for yourself, whether that means staying in the relationship and establishing boundaries, or getting out.

Go back to the beginning of the amplification process and redefine your vision of what a great relationship looks like, because this isn't it. You may need help doing this, because there are some real possibilities that might not seem available to you. A good counselor or therapist can help guide you back into the realm of possibility. As a start, there's a wonderful book by Patricia Evans called *The Verbally Abusive Relationship*, which can help you identify abusive behaviors in your own relationship and get clear about your options.

Measurements that produce good outcomes in well-balanced love relationships include indications of mutual respect, time spent together, and regular conversations about the health of the relationship. You might want to focus on how often you laugh together, and try to push that number up, or measure the number of creative ways you can support each other in achieving your individual visions. The romance dial is a fun one to turn up, by measuring the number of long hand-in-hand walks, or fires lit, or stars counted, or time in bed. You can magnify the feeling of love in your relationship by measuring thoughtful gestures: the little note packed in the lunch box or hidden in the sock drawer, the flowers sent to the office, the secret saving-up for a treasure coveted by your partner.

Once you've got the right context established for your measurement system, and you've selected productive measurements, make those measurements concrete. Check in with your partner on each measure's validity to verify that you're not measuring progress in a vacuum. Measure consistently. If you've agreed that you will treat each other with mutual respect, there's never a time when it's okay not to. It may happen, but the relationship will be better served if the person at fault admits the error and takes steps to reconcile the matter. It will be helpful here, too, if you and your partner have agreed on what those steps are, whether they entail simply a heartfelt apology or an hour's worth of groveling.

Lastly, measure often enough to keep your relationship vision on track. If you and your partner continually catch each other doing the right things, the inverse Zeno effect will kick in and your relationship will blossom. Remember, the couple who measures together finds pleasure together!

9. AMP UP YOUR HEALTH AND APPEARANCE

Creating Your Ultimate Self

KAREN AND I MET EACH OTHER when she was the marketing director of her uncle's commercial printing company, and her uncle's company was a client of mine. Her uncle suggested that I might be a good speaker for an event she was organizing. He also expressed the belief that she and I would make a good match as friends, since she was recently divorced and a single mom, and so was I. He was right.

She and I hit it off right away. We had plenty to talk about regarding the dating scene, raising our children, dealing with difficult ex-husbands, and being powerful women in a world that didn't always appreciate powerful women. I will always remember us sitting under the stars in chairs shaped like giant high-heel shoes, drinks in hand, contemplating the crazy left turns our lives had taken. We did not know how crazy those left turns would get. We didn't know, for example, that ten years later she would be diagnosed with a rare blood disorder that would change her life forever.

Her official diagnosis is acquired agammaglobulinemia, or as she prefers to call it — since she says she can pronounce it — IgG subclass deficiency. The presenting features of most patients with this deficiency are recurrent infections involving the ears, sinuses, nose, bronchi, and lungs. When the lung infections are severe and occur repeatedly, permanent damage to the lungs will occur.

The first symptom she endured as a result of having this disorder was a miscarriage. Of course, she didn't know about the connection then. All she knew was that afterward she experienced an overall feeling of chronic fatigue, chest tightness, trouble breathing, sinus infections, and bronchitis.

"I would go to the doctor and be given an antibiotic, which would make me feel better for a few days, then I would begin feeling sick again," Karen told me. "Each time I saw the doctor, I progressed to a stronger antibiotic. So for one year, it was one long episode that didn't go away. I felt *awful* all the time. I can remember sitting with my husband and crying one night because I felt so bad and just wasn't getting better."

Her low point came during the holidays of 2005. "The day before Thanksgiving I was given a vaccination, and I was in so much pain it felt like my arm had been amputated at the shoulder. Thanksgiving Day, I couldn't move my arm and had gotten no sleep the night before. Luckily, a relative brought a painkiller over and I self-medicated — just put myself to sleep to put me out of my misery. After that, my health just kept getting worse; I progressed to the point where I could hardly breathe, lost my voice, and ended up in bed for a week because I didn't even have the strength to get up."

Karen had a blood test done to rule out lymphoma and spent Christmas worrying about the upcoming results from that test. "I honestly looked like death walking for over a month."

Her illness was a mystery to the doctors she was seeing. It was only when her new primary care physician sent her to a specialist she'd seen before that the pieces began to come together. "Four years before this episode, I'd experienced a miscarriage, had recurrent bronchitis following, and then had been referred by my primary care doctor to an immunologist. She'd given me a vaccination that made my bronchitis go away. I thought I'd been given the miracle drug that took care of the situation, and put it out of my mind as best I could. When I was sent to this specialist again, she immediately knew something more serious was going on."

Like so many people with chronic conditions, Karen had to go through a lot before she received a correct diagnosis for her condition. When she finally did, her relief was mixed with dismay at what it would mean for her and her family.

"When I first began my treatment in January of 2006, it was a monthly blood infusion given to me intravenously at home by a nurse. I would feel great for about three weeks, then I would feel like I was tanking until my next infusion. About a year ago, the FDA approved doing the infusions subcutaneously, or under the skin. Now I'm able to self-administer the infusion each week, and my levels stay more constant."

This means that each Friday Karen preps her bags of blood product, takes a painkiller, inserts three tubes into her abdomen through which she will pump the immunoglobulin replacement into her body, and lies still for one hour. "Then I take the tubes out, which is sometimes very painful. My abdomen looks like an alien creature is going to jump out of it, because it becomes all distorted from the liquid that has just been pumped in. Over the next few days, the lumps go down as the liquid is absorbed into my body and bloodstream. On Saturday, my tummy is still sore and I'm easily fatigued."

Every week, Karen's chronic illness brings a component to her life that she never could have imagined during our talks. Yet what she's done with it continues to amaze me. We go out to dinner periodically, just the two of us, and she shows up beautiful, cracks jokes, enjoys her martini, and is generally the same upbeat Karen I've always known. I asked her about that.

"I'm not upbeat all the time. I've had my moments when I've been angry and sad. But my general nature is to be an optimist. I believe there is a reason this illness is in my life, and that life is too short to go around being angry and sad all the time. I also feel that although I have a chronic disease that will affect me my whole life, it's a treatable one. I'm grateful because the outcome could have been different."

Is Karen amping up her possibilities? I think she is. She's accepted that this condition could be with her forever, and yet refuses to let it dictate how she creates her reality. Is it possible that a cure could be found during her lifetime? Perhaps. But even if not, Karen is making the most of her ability to design her life in a way that accommodates her condition without making it the point.

Her husband and two daughters have not only taken this change in stride but also make a special effort to surround her with a love she calls "amazing." I'm impressed with her family, and I shall forever be embarrassed by the fact that when she first introduced me to her current husband, I told her to run as fast as she could in the other direction. (And perhaps my raw embarrassment stays fresh because, every time we're together, she reminds me of it. [Bad word here.]) I could not have anticipated that the relationship she developed with the man she introduced me to that night — under wacky and difficult circumstances — would be the foundation that Karen's ability to deal with her condition currently rests on. And yet it's clearly so.

I believe that Karen's response to her illness inspires her family and friends to embrace it as part of her. As a result, her life is full of happiness, celebration, gratitude, and love.

I'm not an expert on chronic or terminal conditions. (Except for neck and back pain, maybe.) But as an observer of people with those conditions, I see that some chronic or terminally ill people have chosen to wring from life everything they can — whether this means not giving up on a cure, as in the case of Christopher Reeve, or being a celebrant of life, however that happens to be defined.

Perhaps these people have even more reason than most of us to be firmly grounded in the fact that life is what you make of it. If you are suffering from a chronic or potentially terminal condition, let me say that I'm honored you're reading this book, my heart is with you, and I'm wishing you every possibility.

In this chapter, we explore some examples of people who have overcome addictions, injuries, and illnesses and are doing amazing things with their lives. We'll also talk about some of the more universal health issues, such as weight loss and physical fitness. Wherever you are on the health scale, I believe there are possibilities available to you, and that you can amplify them into reality.

QUITTING

Imagine waking up one morning, putting on your pants, and finding them ridiculously loose. You get brave enough to step on a scale — something you haven't done in a long time — and you discover you've lost . . . fifty pounds!

That's what happened to my friend Joe in his early sixties. He wasn't ill. Quite the contrary. He was healthier than he'd been for most of his adult life. "For a long time in my life," he said, "I couldn't quit anything. Then all of a sudden I started quitting everything. I knew I was at a point in my life when I wasn't going to last much longer. I didn't want to live my life anymore." Joe needed a change in his life, and he needed one right then.

He gave up drinking, smoking, and coffee. Joe had been a very serious drinker. His alcoholic behavior had caused him much grief in his life, including the loss of relationships. After he'd re-mained sober for a while, he turned to the other bad habits in his life. "I gave up coffee because, for me, coffee and cigarettes went together. I knew I'd never be able to quit smoking if I kept drink-ing coffee," he told me.

The day he stepped on that scale was much happier than the day he woke up to discover that all his toes were asleep and stayed that way. His doctor told him he had neuropathy, a nerve disorder that causes pain, numbness, and tingling in various parts of the body. Joe's neuropathy was later linked to diabetes. He was also diagnosed with high cholesterol and high blood pressure. He knew something had to change. "I was the most amazed person when I quit all that stuff," Joe said. "Talking about it every day is what worked. I went to AA meetings every day." (An excellent decoherence technique.)

Soon after he'd given up these bad habits, Joe took up golf as a reward. He bought himself some lessons. In the beginning he walked the course when he played, carrying his bag.

"Really, I walked because I couldn't afford the cart," he said with a grin.

Fifty pounds later, he looked back and knew that all the walk-ing was a big contributor to his weight loss. But he also had a se-cret weapon: cookie dough. "I started making this cookie dough with raisins, real oats, cinnamon, and nutmeg. The recipe called for a cup and a half of brown sugar, but I reduced it to half a cup of brown sugar and half a cup of Splenda. I used to bake the cook-ies, but one day I ate some cookie dough and decided I liked it better than the cookies. I'd eat it every night around eight or nine with half an orange."

Later he sent an email to update me. "I didn't mention that I eat only two meals a day plus the cookie dough and half an or-ange. I'd never lose any weight if I ate three meals plus the cookie dough."

So we can add a meal a day to the things Joe has given up.

"I stopped using sugar too. I lost my taste for it. I'm fortunate because I've always loved to cook, and I love vegetables, so I eat pretty healthily."

Joe's neuropathy has subsided, and he feels enormously better. Besides playing golf, he stays fit by taking long hikes with his dog. He'll probably have to take medication to control his high blood pressure, blood sugar, and cholesterol for the rest of his life. But now he has a life that he wants to live. And he thinks maybe it's time for a new cookie dough recipe.

ACCESSING THE POSSIBILITIES

Can you imagine yourself as a vibrantly healthy individual today? Or would it be great to just stop being sick or overweight or in pain? Joe's vision was about becoming a different person, a person who cared actively about his long-term health. He felt so horrible that almost anything different would have been better. The pain of continuing on his current path had finally become greater than the pain of getting off it. After so many years of drinking and smoking, he had no idea what his life would be like without those things. Rather than imagining a seemingly distant world of beauty and light and perfect health, Joe crafted a vision about finally taking charge of his life, a very short-term vision that would have to be resurrected every day, every hour, and every moment in order to come true. In the many decisions he made each day, Joe would either honor the integrity of his vision or deny it. Today, years after quitting his multiple vices, Joe's vision is intact.

Another friend of mine, Jack, used to say that each of us is a biological experiment. We are born with a certain physical makeup unlike any other person's in the world. Yes, we may have traits passed down to us from our parents and grandparents, even from our ancient ancestors. But ultimately we are individuals with different habits, environments, and events in our lives that help mold our healthy (or unhealthy) natures.

You may be in relatively good health and want to become more athletic. You may be athletic and wish to improve on your personal best. You may be in fair health with a desire to feel better. Or you may be in very poor health, in which case you have a long road ahead and need strength to get through.

Whatever your health situation, you can begin from where you are by creating a clear vision of where you'd like to be. To begin creating that vision, put yourself in wave mode to access more of the possibilities available to you by asking yourself some of the questions in the following sections. Then explore questions of your own that will take you even further.

What Does Being Healthy Look Like to You?

Is it waking up in the morning feeling great? Or running those three miles a minute or two faster? Is it qualifying for the Olympics or exercising three times a week? For many of us in the United States, weighing less is a desirable health goal. (If you want to see how obesity is frighteningly trending upward in our country, visit the website of the national Centers for Disease Control and Prevention at www.cdc.gov and search for "obesity trends." You'll find a graphic showing the recent trends. It's pretty scary!) If you would like to lose weight, how much would you like to lose?

Perhaps to you being healthy is recovering fully from an injury. I personally am investing in physical therapy right now for a crunchy-sounding knee. While I was receiving treatment one day, I met a young woman who had injuries to both her feet. She had no structural integrity on the right side of her body, and her walk of a few steps from the bed to a chair was perhaps even more painful to watch than it was for her to do. She'd been on crutches for months and her dream was simply to be able to walk normally again. She was an athletic woman. In high school she'd been a hurdler. By some of her comments, I could tell she was frustrated and wanted to be well right away. But she also conveyed the fact that she was willing to do whatever it took to get herself back on her feet. She had a vision, and she was going to make it come true.

(Although it was easy to jump to the conclusion that she was injured during some athletic event, the truth was that she'd hurt herself while *dancing with friends*. So be careful out there on the dance floor. Apparently anything can happen.)

If you're a baby boomer like me, you might consider adding "be stronger" to your vision if it's not already in there. Strength training maintains muscle mass, increases bone density, and helps with weight management. As you age, the strength of your muscles will determine how easy it is to sit down or stand up, lift things like grandchildren, and engage actively in the things you love to do. Because strength training increases bone density, it will make you less susceptible to breaks if you should fall. But it also helps you maintain balance, so you have less chance of falling in the first place.

Do you have a flexibility goal? In your vision, perhaps you regularly and joyfully take yoga classes or perform a sunrise stretching routine. How flexible do you want to be? How will you know when you've achieved that level of flexibility?

A vision of health can also include mental health. Would you like more peace in your life, less worry?

When Would You Like to Achieve Your Vision?

If weight loss is part of your vision, by what date will you lose that specified number of pounds? If your goal includes starting a strength-training program, by what date will you start? If you've decided that you'll run a marathon, which one will you run, in what year?

Gauge the Emotional Impact of Your Vision

Are you excited about your vision of glowing health? Does it motivate you? If not, what could you add to make it more compelling? Can you imagine what you will feel like when your vision has come true? Do heads turn to look at you? Do your coworkers notice the change in you? Does your family? What do they say to you, and how does that make you feel? When you wake up in the morning with lots of energy, can you imagine fairly crackling with it, making everything seem easier to do? Does your health vision include workout partners? How does it feel to have that support and motivation there for you? After you work out, does your whole body and brain feel more relaxed and calm? Is it easier for you to access happiness when your health is assured? Do you laugh more?

Record Your Health Vision in Writing and Then Flesh It Out

Find examples of your vision in magazines and cut them out. These might include pictures of the body you'd like to have or the healthy diet you'd like to conform to. Add pictures of people running a marathon or a picture of the medal you'll receive when you've successfully completed it. Look in your local newspaper for activities in which you could participate, such as yoga classes or aquatic exercise classes. Envision all the different ways you could have fun with physical fitness. Could it be a social event for you? Could you and your fitness friends follow a morning workout with a healthy breakfast out on Saturday mornings? How would you mix up your routine to keep it fresh?

AMP IT UP!

I recently ran my first half-marathon: 13.1 miles. Previously, I had never run more than five miles at a time, and that distance not too frequently. I was mostly a two-to-three-mile runner. The training required for a half-marathon includes long runs up to ten miles in length. I looked at that training schedule and thought, "Wow. I wonder if I can do this." Ultimately, there was only one way to find out. I committed to running a particular event with my boyfriend, and then had to commit to that training schedule because I intended to finish and finish well.

Each long training run gave me a feeling of pride. The first time I ran six miles without stopping, I got off the treadmill with a smile on my face. "Yeah," I said silently in my head to all the people working out near me, "I just ran six miles. I rock."

Then I ran eight straight miles. Then ten. At each of these milestones, I reveled in the feeling of pushing myself to do something I'd never done before. My brain registered surprise at each of these accomplishments — apparently, there was still a part of me that wasn't sure I could do it. But there's nothing like actually doing it as proof to yourself, is there? Now I know I can run 13.1 miles in about two hours and twenty minutes. I also know that there's a marathon in my future. I'm not done stretching that dream envelope yet.

What about your dream envelope? Is it big enough? In your hand (or your computer), you now have a written vision of your ultimate state of health. Let's see what we can do to crystallize your focus and make that vision even bigger, bolder, and juicier.

AMP UP YOUR HEALTH! WORKSHEET

What if there were an image of your health that you couldn't see even from your vantage point? Is it possible that you could feel better or accomplish more than you do in the bright picture you portrayed by writing your vision? Use the questions in this worksheet to get a glimpse of that perfectly healthy you. And remember: write down your new ideas as you think of them in order to preserve them (and create a record of your desire in the environment).

The first five questions have to do with physical risk. Just like I had to step out and run that first six miles, something I'd never attempted before, you might need to take some physical risks to create the kind of health you desire. Pick some risks that will stretch — not sprain — your comfort zone. For example, having run five miles before, six miles was a reasonable stretch for me. After I'd run six, then eight became reasonable, and so on. If I'd gotten on the marathon starting line with no training under my belt, no one would call me reasonable anymore. So, use the questions below as thought starters. Choose some risks that will take you out of your comfort zone but not leave you stranded in a bad neighborhood.

1. What's one thing you think you can't do physically? What if you decided to do it anyway?

2. Is there a new sport you could take up? What would it be?

3. If traditionally you've worked out alone, would you consider adding a partner and regularly scheduled workout sessions to your exercise regimen?

4. What investments are you willing to make in your health vision? Buying a piece of exercise equipment for your home? Signing up for a gym membership? Hiring a personal trainer? Visiting a nutritionist? Buying only organic food?

5. Is there someone telling you that you can't achieve your vision of health, that you will always be exactly

as you are? Are you willing to break your dependence on this person's opinion of you and achieve that vision anyway?

People in vibrant health have characteristics and goals that differ from those of people who are not. Here are some of the possibilities that you may not have considered when you created your vision.

6. In your vision, are you "ripped"? That is, can we see your washboard abdominal muscles? Do you have an extremely refined physique?

7. Do you want to teach your children how to live healthy lives; do you want to be a role model for health for them?

8. Could you show others how to care for themselves better, perhaps by teaching exercise classes or becoming a personal trainer?

9. Would you like to enter contests of strength or endurance to test your fitness? What would those be?

10. Can you imagine changing your lifestyle so drastically that people regularly think you are ten or even twenty years younger than you are?

11. Is there a medication, or more than one, you will no longer have to take once your vision becomes a reality?

12. Would you like to accomplish two, three, or even four times more than you were ever able to before because your body can easily keep up? Are people drawn to you because your energy level is so high?

What kinds of fabulous experiences will amping up your health bring to you? Consider the following.

13. Will you find that because you look so great, you are often asked to talk about your area of expertise on television?

14. Would it be exciting if friends who have never asked before invited you to stay at their ski condo? Would you be able to ski the expert runs?

15. Would you go back and play a sport that you gave up years ago because you couldn't play it anymore — and kick everybody's butt?

16. Are there clothes in your closet that you haven't been able to wear for years that now fit like a glove? Are you shopping for new clothes because your others are too big?

17. Is there some mountain in this world that you'd like to climb? A deep wreck you'd like to dive? A cave system you'd like to be able to squeeze through? Some dolphins you'd like to swim with?

18. Would you spend more time in the company of others?

19. Would you book yourself a stay at a health resort that in the past you only allowed yourself to dream about, such as Oprah's reported favorite, Miraval, in Arizona?

20. What would you *stop* doing? What would you erase from your life to make room for your vision of health? You may be thinking about bad habits here, but let me suggest some other things as well, such as hanging around with people whose health habits conflict with your brand-new shiny ones. You might choose to eliminate stress-causing self-talk. Or decide that you'll no longer make your family's unhealthy favorites for dinner. What would *you* leave out?

Because mental health is so much a part of overall health, the emotions you will have as an optimally healthy person are an important part of your vision. Here are some questions you can use to explore the emotional component of the healthier you.

21. Will you be more peaceful because of your excellent health? Will you exude calm?
22. Will you feel a deep, spiritual connection with the universe and everything and everyone in it?
23. Will you use your workout sessions as meditations on the here and now, or as a connection to nature, a time to quiet your mind?
24. Will you joyfully celebrate your physical achievements or your ability to overcome your resistance to the routine?
25. What role will riotous, contagious laughter play in your life? How often do you want to laugh? What emotion would you like to replace with joy?

Great! Now that you've got an amped-up vision, let's work on aligning your beliefs to support your creation process.

BELIEF MANAGEMENT

Joe said he didn't want to live his life anymore the way it was, and that he knew he was headed for bad things — including, potentially, death — if he kept walking down the same path. His primary belief became: "Change is no longer optional. It's necessary." With that belief settled firmly in his bones, he had no choice but to act in accordance with it.

In this way, beliefs and action can drive each other. If your beliefs are aligned with your vision, you will take actions that also are aligned. If you take actions that are aligned with your vision, your beliefs will begin to line up.

To begin this alignment process, set some time aside when you can sit quietly and review your beliefs about your health. You may be unaware of many of them, so this might be more of an introduction than a review. That's okay.

MY HEALTH ALIGNMENT WORKSHEET

BELIEF ALIGNMENT

When we feel challenged, we are usually carrying around a collection of "evidence" that does not serve us. In this first exercise, write down in the "Probability Fragility" column some of the evidence that threatens your vision, and then counter that evidence in the "Possibility Agility" column with some disconfirming evidence that supports the fact that you can break out of the confines of your beliefs about the present. I've given you some examples to get you started.

PROBABILITY FRAGILITY	POSSIBILITY AGILITY
I'll never be able to lose any weight.	Weight loss is a process I can learn.
I don't have time to train for a marathon.	My priorities decide the use of my time.
I have absolutely no discipline.	I am learning discipline today.

ACTION ALIGNMENT

In this exercise, list actions that are part of your regular repertoire, but that won't support your vision. Then list new actions that you'll use to disrupt the ones that aren't working for you. I've given you an example here too.

I DON'T SUPPORT MY VISION WHEN I... don't get enough sleep, and then I get stressed out during the day because I'm so tired,

SO INSTEAD I WILL... be in bed by 10 PM every night, even if I read for a while to help me fall asleep.

I DON'T SUPPORT MY VISION WHEN I... _____

_____ ,

SO INSTEAD I WILL... _____

_____ .

I DON'T SUPPORT MY VISION WHEN I... _____

_____ ,

SO INSTEAD I WILL... _____

_____ .

I DON'T SUPPORT MY VISION WHEN I... _____

_____ ,

SO INSTEAD I WILL... _____

_____ .

I DON'T SUPPORT MY VISION WHEN I... _____

_____ ,

SO INSTEAD I WILL... _____

_____ .

I discovered a really great way to get new beliefs to kick in when you need them: create a brand name for the "You" that you will become when your vision is manifest, a name and image you can call on when you need to refocus your energies in the direction of your dreams. I invented a brand for myself that I call the Possibility Chick. The Possibility Chick believes that every possibility is truly available, that worry is pointless, that people are looking to her to shore up their own belief systems, and that she is a confident creator of her own experience in every moment. When I find myself running old routines in my head, such as beating myself over the head for something I feel I've done wrong, I can pull up and ask myself: "Is this how the Possibility Chick would react?" Almost instantly, my perception of the situation shifts, I feel calmer, and I'm able to turn back and focus on the moment I want to create, rather than on the moment my misguided brain was creating from old information.

You can do the same thing. For example, if you imagine becoming a warrior woman of great power, a goddess of health, you might label that archetypal image of yourself Athena. When you're in a bad place in your head, or you're taking actions not in accordance with your vision, you can ask yourself, "What would Athena do?" Or: "How would Athena act in this situation?"

When we step out of our comfort zones to make our dreams come true, we can't help but be transformed by the process. If you give yourself to this creative process, you'll be a different person at the end, a person with a much larger comfort zone, more confidence, and stronger will.

In your vision of health (or indeed, your vision for your entire life), you should have a picture of the person who brought it all to life. Who is she? How does she deal with daily worries? How does she decide to take one risk and not another? What do other people see when they look at her? What would she project into the world? How does she treat her physical and mental self?

Name her. Is she . . . You the Invincible? You the Triumphant? SuperYou? You 2.0? Maybe the name you give yourself will be something completely different, as in the Athena example above. You can make up a name that conveys the power that this more powerful and confident you possesses.

You know that when you actually become her, you will act differently, speak differently, and focus on different things. Once you have your future self firmly in your mind, when your brain begins to go off on a tangent that doesn't serve you, you can ask yourself this question: "What would I 2.0 do?"

Instantly, you'll know this tangent isn't it. You'll also know what she would do, and you'll be able to do it, in that moment. Make You 2.0 choices, and soon you will *become* You 2.0.

DECOHERE IT

Decoherence is sometimes about *not* doing things. Suppression, a subtle form of creation, becomes the name of your game. The environment can help you amplify your desired possibility if you create a lot of information about it so that it is the strongest and most robust choice out of all possibilities available. At the same time, all the other possibilities must be suppressed. By helping the environment suppress those other possibilities, you can make your desired possibility appear even more powerful by contrast.

If weight loss is one of your goals, for example, you can *increase* exercise in your life, but you can also *decrease* caloric intake. By taking yoga, you can increase flexibility while decreasing stress. If you're suffering from a sports injury, you can increase the amount of rest you get every night while decreasing the amount of high-impact exercise in order to speed recovery and avoid further injury. On the other hand, if the injury is minor, you might choose to take medication to suppress inflammation while increasing exercise intensity or volume to achieve your goals. By increasing your intake of water before meals, you can suppress appetite. The combination of the things you add and those you suppress is what truly brings your health vision to life.

One of my favorite suppression strategies for weight loss is to consume a lot of food but take in fewer calories. You can do this by choosing foods that have a low energy density, which means they have fewer calories but more water and fiber, which fill you up. As you might imagine, vegetables and fruits are generally low energy density foods, but you do have to watch what form you consume them in. For the same number of calories, for example, you can eat either two cups of grapes or a quarter cup of raisins. Which do you think will keep you feeling fuller longer? Other foods you can eat in high volumes, but which have lower energy density, include whole grains, such as brown rice, oatmeal, and popcorn, and legumes, such as beans, peas, and lentils. The more often you choose to eat a lot of these types of foods versus high energy density foods, such as butter, sugar, and so on, the more likely you are to see the pounds melt away.

By repetitively choosing low energy density foods, you'll change your overall diet mix and your body too. By repetitively performing other actions aligned with your health vision, whether those actions are about creation or suppression, you can begin to fire up the decoherence engine. Every time you skip a cigarette, you send a message to the environment and to your brain that your vision has begun to come true. Every time you overcome the warm nest of your bedsheets and strike out on that walk — no matter the weather — again, the decoherence motor begins to spin.

But not only motors spin. All quantum particles also have spin, or what physicists refer to as a particle's "intrinsic angular momentum." What you want to create is the real-life equivalent of a quantum spin field, in which a collection of subatomic particles is polarized so that all are spinning in the same direction. By putting consistent information into the environment in a variety of forms — thought, speech, writing, and action — you begin to craft a reality spin field, as it were, upon which your vision can be woven. When all your creation tools — observation, belief, action, and measurement — are aligned and spinning in the same direction, you effectively polarize yourself and your surroundings. When everything in your life points at your vision, the spin field becomes even stronger, invoking your vision from the ether.

For an example of how to build an ultrastrong reality spin field, consider the story of John "J2" Mryckzo. Paralyzed from the chest down in a high-speed motorcycle accident at the age of nineteen, J2 has not left his love of speed and extreme sports behind just because he's in a wheelchair. He goes trail riding in his chair and has traveled miles in it to see friends. He even jumps ramps. He wants other disabled people to know that life doesn't have to end because of a spinal cord injury.

J2 learned to design websites despite his inability to open his hands, and he started a website called Extremechairing.com, now the largest adaptive-action-and-adventure-sports website in the world. The site shares information about sports participation for those with limited mobility, and has nonprofit status. I was deeply inspired by athletes featured on this site who had accomplished physical feats that I in my able body have not. Could not! I recommend checking out some of the videos.

At the age of twenty-eight, J2 successfully completed an event of his own design, Rollathon 2008, a grueling two-hundred-mile trek in his wheelchair across the state of Illinois. Next he wants to create an all-terrain vehicle replacement for the wheelchair to help the wheelchair-bound go places they have not dreamed of going before. His whole life has become a monument to pushing the envelope, *no matter the circumstances*. For that, J2 has my complete admiration. He may have physical limitations, but I'll tell you what: he sure knows how to amp it up!

APPLYING THE INVERSE ZENO EFFECT

There is only one way I know to lose weight, and that is to measure, measure, measure. After I gave birth to my son — who weighed ten and a half pounds, by the way, speaking of measurements — I found I had a pregnancy weight gain complicated by gestational diabetes (high blood sugar levels that occur during pregnancy). In other words, I had a *lot* of weight to lose. Every day, I measured my caloric intake. I subscribed to a particular kind of diet that prescribed a limited selection of foods, so that my choices were simple. I had a desired end weight in mind, and I weighed myself every day. I achieved my goal in three months. During the time I was on the diet, I was sometimes frustrated, but I also felt clear and focused. Because I surrendered to my mea-suring system, my choices each day about what to eat, how much to eat, and how much exercise to get were all preselected, and I simply followed the system.

On another occasion, I used my journal to help me measure my progress toward my weight loss goal. I weighed myself every day; recorded what I ate, how many calories I consumed, and how much exercise I did; and then plotted my weight daily on a line graph. Pictures speak to me much louder than numbers, so the graphical representation of my progress was revealing. By watching that line go up and down, I began to see how diet, sleep, stress, and exercise all interacted with one another to affect my weight. Over time, cyclical changes became noticeable, such as the monthly effect of my hormones. Ultimately, the line began a steady downward progression and I achieved my goal. *The downward trend of the line alone motivated me to maintain the trend*. I did not want to see that line go up!

Measurement creates focus. By focusing on our contributions to either the creation of our health vision or the status quo, we can begin to take corrective action. When the impact of that corrective action appears in our measurements, those measurements then become motivational themselves. That's when the inverse Zeno effect kicks in.

So, how can you start a measurement system for your health vision that will help you bring it to life? First, remember that the system you are creating is designed to support and gently guide you, not punish you. With that and your vision in mind, set your baseline — or beginning — measurement and your end measurement. In other words, where are you now, and where will you be once your vision is manifest? For example, if weight loss is part of your vision, record how much you weigh now and how much you will weigh on the target date. If strength improvement is desirable, then record how much weight you can lift or press with various muscles or muscle groups, and how much you would like to be able to lift or press by your target date. If flexibility is your goal, record how close you can get to touching your toes, for example, and how much closer you'd like to get.

If stress reduction is your goal, you can use a measure such as the Hassle Scale to set a baseline for yourself. (Yes, there's actually a Hassle Scale! And you can find it on my website at www.PossibilitiesAmplified.com under "Resources.") The Hassle Scale is designed to help you pinpoint the negative events in your life that might be causing you stress, and how much each event has impacted you. If your goal is to reduce the toll of stressful events in your life, then measuring your responses to them monthly (or even weekly) will provide indispensable information on how well you're doing.

Another tool you can use to set a baseline is a website called AmIHealthy.com (available at the time of this writing). Once you register there, you can take a health survey that will compare your subjective responses about your health to the responses of others with similar conditions. At the end of the survey, you'll receive a report that you can share with your doctor and use to track the success of your health program over time.

The great thing about measuring health is that there is a plethora of health measurement instruments available and ready for you to use, whether your vision includes reducing your blood sugar, living independently, recovering from an injury, or lowering your cholesterol. To find them, you can search the Internet for terms such as *health measurement*, or visit your local bookstore.

CAUTION

Not every website on the Internet provides reliable, unbiased information. When beginning your search, choose websites that end in ".gov" or ".edu." Those sites are government and university sites, which are likely to offer validated material. And always check with your doctor before making changes in your health routine.

Because you're working with your own personal measuring system, you might think that you have to go it alone, but you don't. The Internet can also provide you with a support system. Online communities engaged in bringing particular health visions to life are readily available. HealthCentral.com provides online communities that focus on health issues ranging from acid reflux to smoking cessation. On the message boards there, you'll be able to read about what others are going through and how they've created success, and participate in the conversation. Online support in this form is available twenty-four hours a day. And who knows? You might just inspire someone else who needs it.

TRACKING YOUR PROGRESS

Once you've got your baseline and endpoint established, set a time line and define some milestones. By what date do you want your health vision to be fully realized? How will you know you're on track as time passes?

To make sure you stay on target over time, specify some interim measurements. Let's stick with our weight loss example. If your vision is to be a lean, mean, sexy machine in three months, and this means a weight loss of ten pounds, then you'll need to lose an average of just under a pound a week to reach your goal. A milestone at four weeks would be the loss of between three and four pounds. If you're in that range at four weeks, it's time to party! If you're outside that range, then perform a simple recalibration of your measurement system to put yourself back on track. I would *not* reset subsequent milestones. The idea is to fine-tune your performance (behavior or choices) gently and compassionately so that you can still hit them. Every pound you lose, every inch closer you get to your toes, each additional step you take, will be a celebration of the possibility amplifier within you.

10. AMP UP YOUR GIVING AND COMMUNITY CONNECTION

Enhancing the Two-Way Flow of Gifts

WOULD YOU WORK IN A JOB FOR THIRTY-TWO YEARS of your life *without pay?* Ruth Crawford did. When I interviewed Ruth, she'd recently resigned her post as executive director of the Shiloh Comprehensive Community Center at the age of ninety-two. Thirty-two years prior, after she retired from her thirty-eight-year career as an elementary school teacher in Augusta, Georgia, her attention turned toward home. She became distressed at the condition of her neighborhood.

"I wanted to get rid of the drugs in my neighborhood," Ruth said. "I saw all these little girls and boys staying out so late at night and shooting up their arms. I used to go out there with a stick and break up the groups, you know!"

It doesn't surprise me. At ninety-three, Ruth has an energetic and vibrant spirit, and her humility and sense of humor make her a delightful companion. Ruth told me the story of how she converted the abandoned orphanage across the street from her home into the thriving community center it is today.

"The place was so dilapidated that they put the orphans into private homes, so it was just sitting there empty. A lawyer asked me, 'You don't have any money; how are you going to put something into it?' And I said, 'I've got my brains, and I'm going to use everything in there.'" In a conspiratorial aside to me she added, "The truth is, I operated for one year illegally without a license."

I asked her how she decided that making a success out of that community center was something she could do. She said, "I had nothing but determination and my own desire to fight crime in my neighborhood."

With nothing but passion and purpose, Ruth Crawford has indeed gotten rid of the drugs in her neighborhood. Her community center provides the youth and the elderly in her neighborhood a place to congregate, learn, and connect.

You'd think that'd be enough, but in addition to founding and managing the community center, Ruth's also written three books. Her last book is titled *Peace, Power, and Purpose of Volunteering*. All of Ruth's books are self-published, and she's sold them herself over the years to supplement her income. If you'd like to buy a copy of *Peace, Power, and Purpose of Volunteering*, just send me an email at kim@possibilitiesamplified.com. Ruth'd be happy to mail you one. I asked her about the book.

"I'm not a writer," she said demurely. I suggested that having authored three books, perhaps she was. She said, "I taught elementary school, and so that means your vocabulary is not as sophisticated as if you were teaching high school or college."

Isn't she cute? I asked her what else she'd gotten out of volunteering, besides the benefits the title of her book suggests. "Oh!" she said. "I've made such great friends. I get calls and letters all the time. The last three mayors have been down to see me."

Lastly, I questioned Ruth about the peace that volunteering has brought her. Was she a worrier before? She answered, "You know, when you're helping others, you don't have time to worry."

And that, my friends, is sage advice. Charitable giving is about donating time and resources to those who need it and the organizations that serve them, but what Ruth's story demonstrates is that it also has an amazing and fabulous reciprocal effect. The energy you pour into charitable efforts comes cascading back to you.

Here's a list of twenty-five things your charitable and philanthropic efforts can do for you (and I'm sure this is an incomplete list):

1. Improve your love life.
2. Get you new business.
3. Improve your social life.
4. Connect you with your city's most powerful people.
5. Alleviate depression.
6. Lengthen your life.
7. Provide validation of the importance of your existence.
8. Give you a whole new posse to run with.
9. Help you to remember your highest aspirations.
10. Increase your self-esteem.
11. Improve your physical health.
12. Decrease pain.
13. Hone your negotiation skills.
14. Give you a reason to love yourself when you're struggling.
15. Improve your functional ability in your elder years.
16. Build your children's character.
17. Reduce your tax bill.
18. Get you a new job.
19. Develop your leadership skills.
20. Keep you connected to the universe.
21. Help you learn to salsa.
22. Introduce you to new restaurants.

23. Give you the power to change your community.
24. Let you see the world through new eyes.
25. Help you get the big picture.

Did any of those benefits come as a surprise to you? Let me tell you some of the personal reasons behind how I know these benefits exist. Through my volunteering as a mentor in a minority fellowship program for an industry organization, I met the love of my life. After I left the corporate world, I received job offers from people I'd met through my philanthropic endeavors, as well as consulting opportunities. Through my work as a board member for a nonprofit organization, I received invitations to parties, met powerful people I would otherwise never have met, and even got set up on blind dates by those people. I learned about board governance and the obligations of board membership, which is useful in the business world. When my son set his heart on attending Virginia Tech, I was able to reach out to fellow board members for letters of reference and introductions. When I've felt down, I have lifted my spirits by providing service to the charitable organizations I am involved with.

Although I've lived in my community for thirty years, I learned more about how it works after getting philanthropically involved than I had known in all the years prior. Currently, my company is engaged in supporting the launch of an important project for a nonprofit organization that has far-reaching implications and will change the face of my community. We're amplifying possibility on a large scale. Being a part of something with so much impact is enormously rewarding. There has simply been no end to the tangible and personal benefits I have received from my own charitable efforts and through my participation in the philanthropic efforts of others.

Erika Flora, a project management consultant I met while writing this book, is a powerful evangelist for the benefits that volunteering and philanthropy provide. Erika says, "Giving back has provided me with new skills, strengthened weaknesses, given me a strong sense of purpose, and introduced me to tons and tons of really cool people that I would have never met otherwise: industry contacts, customers, vendors, and friends."

Laura Thrower, education coordinator for an association, describes philanthropy this way: "It teaches you a level of compassion and empathy that I did not experience even as a nurse. It changes your view on the world as a whole, resulting in a completely different view on politics and the community in which we live. I appreciate life, people, and the world so much more."

There are great business results too, as evidenced by this quote from *America's Best*, a magazine for the small business owner. "I can tell you that participating in charity has truly had a positive effect on our bottom line," said Lisa Owens, vice president of San Antonio–based advertising agency Regnier Valdez and Associates. "We got about ten strong prospective client calls when people read about us giving back to community organizations. We actually had five of our clients come out to one of the events that we held for a local charity."

I must tell you that for most of my life I had only a glimpse of the fact that charitable giving and its big brother, philanthropy, could be so influential. I never knew there was such a huge inside world of people and money trying to elevate the lives of others in my community. I was amazed to discover how well developed this inside world is, and more important, that there was a clearly designated place for me in it as a powerful contributor. And there's a place for you too, no matter what your charitable involvement has been to date.

In my youth, I was a charitable dabbler. My participation probably began at the behest of my mother, a staunch feminist. I became a member of the National Organization for Women

(NOW) at the tender age of thirteen. That year, my mother sent me to the NOW national convention in Orlando, Florida, with a few of her friends, since she had to work and was unable to attend. I was the youngest woman attending. As the youngest, I became the conference's mascot and was assigned some really cool things to do. Jack Carter, Jimmy Carter's eldest son, and his wife, Elizabeth, were attending and speaking at the conference. It was my job to fetch the Carters from their hotel room and bring them to the various press conferences and other events in which they were participating. When I think back on it now, I can't imagine what the Secret Service agents must have thought of me when I timidly knocked on the Carters' door.

Over the years, I became a regular contributor to a variety of charities important to me, changing the list periodically as my own values and life changed. I didn't give huge amounts of money, but as the years passed, I have narrowed my giving focus to just a few organizations and upped my donations. Ultimately though, it has been the investment of my *time* that has had the biggest impact on me, because of the valuable relationships I created by doing so.

Beyond my personal experience, study after study has demonstrated that giving through service has positive benefits for almost everyone, particularly as we age.[1] In fact, it seems that those who provide service to others live longer than the recipients of such service.[2] Volunteers report greater life satisfaction and better physical health than those who do not volunteer.[3] They even feel happier and better about themselves than nonvolunteers.[4] In other words, you can amp up your life big time by volunteering!

These very personal benefits are layered on top of the impact you will have on your community, on a charitable organization, and in the lives of those served. This multilayered cake of giving is simply waiting for you to partake of it.

ACCESSING THE POSSIBILITIES

I recently made the decision to tie my company to CARE, a charitable organization that focuses on women and their power to lift whole families and communities out of poverty. You may have seen their "I am powerful" ads. I made this decision because I believe that with self-empowerment comes economic empowerment, with economic empowerment comes political power, and with political power comes the opportunity for reform. I'm clear that part of my vision and life's purpose is the lifting up of women around the world. The plight of women in places like Afghanistan, where women have suffered under the Taliban; Guatemala, where women have been murdered in vast numbers, and convictions for those murders are not forthcoming; and even here in the United States, where the FBI estimates a woman is beaten by her husband or partner every fifteen seconds, resonates deeply with me.

Do you have a cause that resonates with you?

There are innumerable causes that need your support. If you aren't currently involved in a charitable organization or mission, or you are not sure which cause should get your attention, then the first step is choosing the cause that has the most meaning for you. Engaging in a personally meaningful cause can be so incredibly enriching that you will easily find inspiration for your continued involvement. This is your opportunity to change the world! What change would you like to see?

To get you started, here are some online resources that can help you find out more about charitable organizations: how they are run, where they spend their money, and on what causes they primarily focus.

CharityNavigator.org calls itself America's largest charity evaluator. On this site, you can search for a charity by keyword or name. You'll also find tips on being a savvy donor, studies on charitable organizations, and more.

GuideStar.org requires that you log in to conduct a basic search, and has several for-pay options for professional researchers. The basic search, however, is free.

Give.org is brought to you courtesy of the Better Business Bureau. The Bureau provides additional guidance by awarding national charity seals. Charities that meet their Standards for Charity Accountability can display the seal on their websites and printed materials.

If the idea of searching through the thousands of charities out there to find one that suits you doesn't appeal to you, there are some alternatives. You can ask your friends what charities they support with their time and money. (Volunteering together will make it that much more fun.) I got involved with a community theater this way and enjoyed attending the various productions. It is an unfortunate fact that some of your friends support the causes they do because they personally have been touched by specific difficulties in their own lives or in the lives of those they love. A friend of mine who is a breast cancer survivor always organizes a group of us to participate in the Susan G. Komen Race for the Cure. I can't think of a better reason to support a cause than because it will help save the lives of your friends!

If you belong to a religious organization, you're in luck, because they're charities as well as centers of faith. Your church or synagogue will likely have numerous ideas for how you can serve. At my church, I've sung in the choir, designed the church resource book, helped to build a house with Habitat for Humanity, and been a member of a committee to build a new website. I got to do the things I'm good at, have fun, and help.

Some cities have organizations designed to help you help out when you can, without burdening you with an ongoing commitment to any particular organization. The projects are usually only a half day or a full day in length, and you can sign up to participate in just the ones you want. Hands On Miami is such an organization. They require a short orientation, which is held at places like the local bookstore to make it easy for people to attend. Through their website, I was able to sign up to spend a day holding neglected babies, a day pulling up nonnative plants in a state park, and a day cleaning up the streets in a poor urban neighborhood. My son, who needed community service points for school, was able to do some of those things along with me. I was happy to provide him with the experience of helping others in tangible ways.

Your place of work may organize charitable participation as well. As a leader, I have signed up my team to pick up garbage on the beach, and once I joined a volunteer team to build a new mulch path around the gorilla exhibit at the zoo.

Do you now have an idea of some problems you'd like to help solve? And let me say that it's not necessary to limit yourself to just one. You might be as driven to teach children financial literacy as you are to improve the lives of the elderly.

But let me acknowledge another possibility as well: your plate may be so full that you can't imagine adding one more thing to it. I have two answers to that. The first is: then let it go. If a punishing schedule makes volunteering seem impossible to you right now, that's okay. You can always come back to it later. You may be one of the many people today sandwiched between full-time care for aging parents and full-time care for young children, and a full-time job. In other words, you're already doing everything you can do for the community of your family. It might entail working and going to school at the same time. It might be a grueling business travel schedule that has your health taxed and your family upset. The weight of life waxes and wanes, so later might be a better time. Perhaps holding off on the service and contributing financially for now would be a better option.

The second answer I have takes me back to the time when I discovered I was pregnant. I was so busy! I was running a household, going to school, and holding down a full-time job that included travel across five states. How would I *ever* fit a baby in? Well, you parents out there know what happened. I just did. The baby came and something else went out. School was one of those things. It took me years finally to finish my degree. But the rest of the sacrifices and changes I made I have no recollection of. What I do remember is that I had a new joy in my life that expanded my world. I discovered a new role for myself — motherhood — and the attendant responsibilities and rewards of that role positively influenced who I am and what I think is important.

Volunteer work can do the same thing. It can take you out of yourself and your current situation in ways that you can't imagine. Perhaps it becomes the way that you get out of the house every once in a while. Or the way you spend time with your kids. Or how you learn to manage a team. Or how you meet new friends. Laura Thrower told me, "Recently I went through a period where my family needs were pulling at me to the point that I seriously considered resigning from the board of the Kaylen Foundation. However, I became sad at the thought of not being involved in community work. I had a serious chat with my family and explained how important this is to me, and so everyone is trying to be more understanding."

Only you know your own capacity. Please do not take these ideas and feel guilty if it still seems impossible! You are the expert on your life. Whatever you decide is the right answer.

If you are currently involved in a charitable organization or more than one, you are well on your way to accessing the possibilities associated with charitable giving. You may have already experienced some of the benefits that I listed earlier in this chapter. What we'll do in this portion of the chapter is draw out all the possibilities that might exist and capture them in writing.

Visualize Your Participation

How involved would you like to get? Is a visit every month to the senior citizen's center enough, or do you want to get involved in the governance of a charitable organization by being on the board? Might you join or chair a committee, or do you prefer being on the front lines and personally helping the needy?

What does successful participation look like to you? Is it simply being there every week and ladling soup into a bowl with a smile, or is it galvanizing your community to make much-needed change? Perhaps you'll feel the most satisfaction by promoting legislation to support your cause or by joining a speaker's bureau to tell people about it. It might be absolutely critical to have your volunteer work support your industry so that you can meet people who might also provide you with business contacts. You get to define what it means.

Look Out into the Future

Imagine yourself ten years from now or on your deathbed. When you look back at this time of your life, what will you want it to have meant? What greater good did you foster in the world? How did you widen your experience by engaging more fully in your community? What kind of person are you spiritually because of what you gave?

Set a Deadline

If you are not currently involved in a charitable effort, when will you begin? You can set a date by which you will choose the organization or effort to align yourself with. You can set up a donation schedule. Perhaps if you've only donated money, you will set a date by which you will perform your first volunteer service.

Envision the Emotional Impact of Your Giving

The emotional side of your vision will provide the inspiration for your involvement. What kinds of feelings do you want to generate inside yourself through your charitable giving? Will you feel proud? Grateful? Fulfilled? Will your self-esteem improve? Will you feel more loved or more loving? Will you become more humble by seeing up close the circumstances others are forced to live with? Will a feeling of grace pervade your days? Sharon Gelman, executive director of Artists for a New South Africa, says she is able to more truly and deeply enjoy the beauty and opportunity in the world when she is helping to address the problems, injustices, tragedy, and pain in it.

What will be your emotional upside for giving back?

AMP IT UP!

Earlier in this book, I told you the story of Seth Warren and Tyler Bradt, two extreme sportsmen who planned an endless summer, a surfing and kayaking trip around the world following the seasons, and combined that with the philanthropic mission of educating the world about biofuels. To make your vision even more compelling, we can explore ways to merge charitable giving and philanthropy with your other missions and goals. Charity can be woven into your work life, your family life, and your spiritual life. It can be a part of your wealth creation plan.

In the following worksheet, we'll explore some of the ways to amp up your vision of the impact you can have on the world, and how the world will return all that value to you.

AMP UP YOUR GIVING! WORKSHEET

The first set of questions is designed to help you think differently about the way you give and to offer you some food for thought on how to shift or enhance the mental model you have of charitable contribution.

1. If you can't afford a single large gift, could you offer a regular monthly payment year-round? Sustainability of gifts received is an important benefit to charitable organizations.

2. Do you have any noncash assets you could donate, such as items you no longer use or want that would be of value to someone else?

3. Could you host a party, set a cover charge, and give the profits to your favorite charity?

4. Could you host a party to introduce your friends and associates to your favorite charity and its mission? Could you be brave enough to ask them for a commitment at the end?

5. Have you considered microloans? Organizations such as Kiva.org provide very small loans to entrepreneurs, and the person-to-person nature of the loan makes them very rewarding.

6. What kind of volunteer activity would touch your soul or refresh your spirit? Would it be working with children, being out in nature, or helping someone through a difficult situation that you've experienced yourself?

7. Do you have a special skill that would benefit your charity, such as bookkeeping, web design, or marketing

expertise? Volunteering your time and skill will allow you to help in specific and familiar ways.

8. Could your family or business sponsor a specific charity as a group, thereby creating tighter bonds between family members or employees?

9. Charities often use auctions to raise funds. Do you have a product or service that your charity could use as an auction item? Could you commit to donating a certain percentage of the sales of a particular product or service? Can you envision the goodwill and promotional impact of doing so?

10. Does your charity offer philanthropic vacations that would allow you to travel the world, make new friends, and give back at the same time?

11. If you're looking to expand your business nationally or internationally, could you participate in the national or international conferences held by your charity and make helpful connections in other communities?

12. Does your charity have a fund-raising event that will help you get in shape, such as a bike race or marathon, and let you achieve two goals at once?

Now, what if the charitable giving of your time and money provided you with the biggest return you could imagine? What would that look like?

13. Would your circle of friends include more people you admire or have longed to know? Would it be much bigger? Would your life be full of people who love and admire you?

14. Would you win awards that honor your contributions, and would you often appear in local newspapers and magazines as a result?

15. Would your business or career flourish as a result of expanding your network through your philanthropy? Would you receive many more referrals and spend less time cold-calling? Would funding magically appear when you need it? Would advice?

16. What would you learn about yourself that would turn out to be priceless?

17. How would your volunteering fit in with the rest of your life? Would it be easy and natural? Would it be the reason you get out of bed in the morning?

18. What if your giving made a powerful, long-lasting effect on your community or another community that you care about? What problem could you help to completely solve and make go away?

19. Would your charitable work bring your family closer? Would it instill in your teenage children the spirit of giving?

Lastly, the following questions will help you paint the ultimate emotional landscape that will result from your charitable involvement.

20. Do you wake up every day with focus and a sense of purpose?

21. Do you feel more connected to your community, other people, or yourself?

22. Is your soul nurtured? Do you feel deeply spiritual? Does your relationship with your Higher Power deepen?

23. Are you amazed at what you're capable of accomplishing? Are you amazed that it all worked out so well?
24. Are you proud of the impact of your giving?
25. Do you feel more centered, more at peace? More powerful? More grateful?

As you can see from these questions, there's so much that philanthropy gives back. Just as in every other area of your life, I encourage you to have a big, bold, juicy vision of what you intend to create. The development of the vision alone — choosing specific possibilities — is the first step in the Possibility Amplification Process.

Your time on this planet is limited, and the life you live will be the one you create, so why not create the biggest, most beautiful one you can imagine? If you're going to spend your time learning to mold, focus, and direct your energy, you might as well have something gorgeous when you're done.

BELIEF MANAGEMENT: A TALE OF OPTIMISM

Charitable involvement begins with the belief that your contribution will make a difference. I can unequivocally say that it will.

How can I be so sure? Because at the very minimum your giving activities will make a difference in *you*. Ruth Crawford found peace, power, and purpose through her service, all inwardly focused benefits that at first blush don't seem to have much to do with the recipients of that service. Yet we know that's not true. We know that giving changes us, and that those changes are evident and palpable to the people around us.

Mother Teresa, who gave her whole life to service, was one of the most compelling and admired people on the planet in her time here. It has been said of her that she was a source of perpetual joy. When we radiate joy, peace, purpose, and power, the people in our sphere can feel it. It lifts them up. It makes them want to be better people. In our moments of greatest self-connectedness, we inspire those around us to strive for the same. If your only goal in giving is to create that change in yourself, you will have made a difference in this world that extends beyond you.

You may have bigger beliefs about what you can accomplish with your giving, just as Abay, an Ethiopian woman from the Afar tribe, did. I share her story as a result of the work of Phil Borges, a photographer whose projects are focused on the welfare of indigenous and tribal people. Abay's story appears in his book *Women Empowered: Inspiring Change in the Emerging World*. This is Abay's story, from Phil Borges's website.

> Abay was born into a culture in which girls are circumcised before age 12. When it came time for her circumcision ceremony, Abay said, "No." Her mother insisted: An uncircumcised woman would be ostracized and could never marry, Abay was told. When her mother's demands became unbearable, she ran away to live with a sympathetic godfather. Eight years later, Abay returned to her village and began work as a station agent [for CARE], supervising the opening of a primary school and a health clinic and the construction of a well. After five years, she finally convinced one of the women to let her film a circumcision ceremony. She showed the film to the male leaders. They had never seen a female circumcision and were horrified. Two weeks later, the male leaders called a special meeting and voted fifteen to two to end female circumcision in their village.[5]

Abay said no when she was only eight. Her twenty-year journey to abolish the practice of female circumcision in her own tribe was just the beginning. An organization was formed to abolish the practice in other tribes as well. Men and women discussed the issue together. A woman was even elected as leader. In a world where women had not been allowed to participate in any leadership decisions, suddenly women had the power to create a change in policy that directly affected them. Women's voices were heard, and those voices made a difference. Abay's work has changed the fabric of her people's culture for all time. This is no small legacy for an eight-year-old girl who said no.

Do you believe you have the ability to create significant change? Do you believe your passion and purpose alone can change the world or at least your own corner of it? Let's take a look at some of the beliefs you might hold about yourself, the world, and your ability to contribute.

MY GIVING ALIGNMENT WORKSHEET

When we feel challenged, we are usually carrying around a collection of "evidence" that does not serve us. In this first exercise, write down in the "Probability Fragility" column some of the evidence that threatens your vision, and then counter that evidence in the "Possibility Agility" column with some disconfirming evidence that supports the fact that you can break out of the confines of your beliefs about the present. I've given you some examples to get you started.

PROBABILITY FRAGILITY	POSSIBILITY AGILITY
I don't have a lot of money to give.	Any donation I can make helps.

| Nothing I do will make a difference. | My service will affect those around me. |
| The world can't be fixed. | Not unless we try. |

PROBABILITY FRAGILITY	**POSSIBILITY AGILITY**
_____	_____
_____	_____
_____	_____
_____	_____

ACTION ALIGNMENT

In this exercise, list actions that are part of your regular repertoire, but that won't support your vision. Then list new actions that you'll use to disrupt the ones that aren't working for you. I've given you an example here too.

I DON'T SUPPORT MY VISION WHEN I . . . buy into the fact that significant change is hard to come by,

SO INSTEAD I WILL . . . focus on what I can do here and now to make a difference.

I DON'T SUPPORT MY VISION WHEN I . . . _____

_____ ,

SO INSTEAD I WILL . . . _____

_____ .

I DON'T SUPPORT MY VISION WHEN I . . . _____

_____ ,

SO INSTEAD I WILL . . . _____

_____ .

I DON'T SUPPORT MY VISION WHEN I . . . _____

_____ ,

SO INSTEAD I WILL . . . _____

_____ .

I DON'T SUPPORT MY VISION WHEN I . . . _____

_____ ,

SO INSTEAD I WILL . . . _____

_____ .

As in previous chapters, create a plan for supporting the embedding of your new beliefs via meditation, affirmation, journaling, or some of the other tools provided.

DECOHERE IT

Decoherence is the process of strengthening your possibilities by creating a lot of information about them in the environment via your thoughts, words, and actions. As you formulate a vision of your charitable participation, the mental choices you make are strengthening certain possibilities over others. If you've written down your vision for giving, you've made those possibilities even stronger. If you've written them down and shared them publicly, as I have in this book with my public declaration of my support for CARE, you've made them even more powerful.

You can create verbal records that tell the universe your possibilities are powerful by standing up for your beliefs in conversation and by sharing your opinion and support. Many organizations have speakers' bureaus, whose members speak at public gatherings on behalf of the charity. As a member of my local Red Cross speakers' bureau, for example, I've shared the compelling story of the Red Cross with local Rotary clubs and other organizations, as well as with service providers from around the world. Giving just one talk shares your dream of supporting an important organization with many people all at once.

To become a member of a charity's bureau, you must of course begin by volunteering for that organization. This brings us to the ultimate decoherence techniques for giving: donating and volunteering. Even if you start small — a small amount of time or a small amount of money — your ultimate philanthropic vision begins to coast on those wheels. If you've never given before, you instantly become "a giver." That's a huge step. If you're a regular giver and want to amp it up, then the way you give, what you give, and who you give to — as defined by your vision — will be significantly more powerful than how much you've given to date.

Why? Because by operating from your vision and your specific desired results, you combine *giving* with *focus*. Focus is a specific form of observation. As I discussed in chapter 1, observation alone changes outcomes. When you apply focus, you apply observation like a laser. It's as if you're using the same amount of available light, but you're concentrating it and amping up the intensity by a significant order of magnitude. When you do so, both you and your selected cause or causes benefit exponentially. (This is also true, by the way, whenever you get clear and apply focus in a particular direction.)

Let me direct you to a great website: VolunteerMatch.org. At this site you can search for volunteer opportunities that may be perfectly suited to you. At the time of this writing, VolunteerMatch tells me that in my city I can sign up to become an adult literacy volunteer, help out at a local museum, or work with at-risk kids. This is just one way to find specific options in your community.

Still not sure what actions to take? If you're having trouble getting to the "volunteer and/or donate" stage, there are probably a couple of reasons why. First, you haven't really gotten clear about what causes and charities you want to focus on. Second, you're afraid to jump in. Remember, at the very beginning people get stuck when applying decoherence because such actions and uses of our time seem foreign to us. You might feel like the Tin Man in the movie *The Wizard of Oz*, rusted stiff from years of being out in the rain. It was the judicious application of the oilcan that helped the Tin Man move freely again.

You can apply the oilcan to your own squeaky charitable joints by doing simple things, like buying a T-shirt from your charity's website or donating five dollars online. (No interaction with people! Safe!) Once you've got your knees going again, you might want to pay a visit to the charitable organization you wish to support. This is a great way to help with the first reason you may have been unable to act, the unclear vision.

Your visit should reveal a few things:

1.   You like or don't like the people involved. If you can feel the heart of the organization just by being in the presence of its staff and volunteers, then you will find it easier to make your commitment. You'll remember why you wanted to start giving in the first place. If your interactions leave you cold, you'll know it's time to move on.

2.   You get a clear sense of mission, or instead a taste of what I call "fuzzy future syndrome": a condition in which there does not seem to be a clear definition or understanding of the organizational vision. You'll want to be part of an organization that's strongly attached to its purpose and knows where it's heading.

3. There's either easy camaraderie between workers or strained relationships. It is an unfortunate truth that charitable organizations are often stretched beyond capacity. This can lead to long hours and a cranky disposition in many of its employees. But do the employees genuinely seem to like each other? If the environment seems competitive or bitter, beware. (On the other hand, if your specialty is human resource management, dive on in! This is the place for you.)

No organization is perfect, but one that feels right to you is more likely to make you happy about your time spent serving it.

For most of us, it's the specter of an enormous time commitment that terrifies us to death. We're afraid of what they will ask of us, we're afraid we'll take on too much, and we're afraid that we won't be able to say no. If these are your concerns, then let me refer you back to the twenty-five benefits I listed earlier in this chapter, and the comments from others regarding their payback.

I admit that when I'm personally asked to step up for something else, my brain goes into "panicked restructuring" mode. But so far, I've usually been able to say yes, and I still feel as if I'm getting the best part of the bargain. My philanthropic commitments have made my personal life richer and my business and career more successful. And I'm willing to bet five bucks that if you surveyed your charitably involved friends, they'd say the same thing. (Send your survey results to kim@possibilitiesamplified.com. I'm always looking for positive stories.)

Know that volunteering for an organization is not necessarily a lifetime commitment. (Although there *are* some women in my local Red Cross chapter who have been members for over forty years! Wouldn't it be great to give your energy for that many years to an organization that meant that much to you?) At times you'll need to move on because of other commitments or a desire to shift the focus of your commitments. Every organization understands that life is full of change, including a reconsideration of one's choice to volunteer. Although they may express disappointment or sadness at your leaving, mostly they will feel grateful that you offered help at all.

You, a willing volunteer, are a precious commodity. Don't let fear hold you back from getting all the benefits of giving.

APPLYING THE INVERSE ZENO EFFECT TO GIVING

"It's not enough." If I could pluck one negative measurement out of your mind, mouth, and heart, this would be it. Once you develop the mindset that lets you help, and as a result you start to focus on where to volunteer, it's easy to be overwhelmed by how much there is to fix in the world. That daunting fact alone stops many people from ever getting started. Allowing your eyes to be opened more to the plight of those around you can result in spiritual pain that sometimes seems too much to bear. However, allowing yourself to see the worst possible outcomes will also reveal the ways that you can help. By creating and putting into action a charitable decoherence plan, you can begin to assuage that spiritual pain by feeling as if you're having an impact.

If you refuse to judge yourself regarding the natural limits on your ability to give (such as income, financial and time obligations, being human, and so on), you can then begin to create a personal measurement system for your charitable efforts that will accelerate the effects of your giving. These effects will be felt not only by the recipients of your giving but by you as well.

Here's a list of some suggested places to notice and measure your progress that will activate the inverse Zeno effect and accelerate your efforts as you begin the process of giving (if you already give your time or money, go on to the next list).

1. Record the moment you decided to become a giver. Write it in your journal. Celebrate it.
2. Choose a charitable organization(s) to support.
3. Complete your charitable giving plan.
4. Find the address to which you'll mail your donation, or the web page where you can do it online.
5. Read about volunteer opportunities.
6. Talk to a friend about your decision to give or about the organization you've chosen to support.
7. Decide what percentage of your income you will donate each year, the amount you will give every month, or the amount you will give one time. (Note that it's not about the amount or the frequency, it's about making the decision.)
8. Review your personal history as a giver. Perhaps you loaned a classmate your gold crayon in elementary school. Maybe you cleared the table for your mom without being asked, taught a coworker a computer shortcut, or let someone cut in front of you at the grocery store. You'll probably find something altruistic you did in the previous week, if not the previous day!
9. Make your first donation.
10. Sign up as a volunteer or for volunteer training.

If you already give and you're looking to amp up the two-way flow of gifts, here are some places you can catch yourself doing something good and Zeno it:

1. Call one of your volunteer buddies and ask her out to lunch. The closer such relationships get, the more likely they are to bear fruit, both for you and for your

charity. Not to mention the value you will bring to your volunteering buddy.

2. Spend five minutes visualizing how your gift has helped someone in need or remembering a time when your charitable organization of choice performed in a stellar fashion in part because of your gifts.

3. Say yes to a social invitation arising from your charitable service.

4. If your charitable organization gives awards to philanthropists in your community or to volunteers, nominate one of your friends for an award.

5. Consider and read up on a charitable vacation. For example when I was younger, I wanted to go with Earthwatch and tag mountain lions in Idaho. Now I think I'd rather go teach business skills to women in Guatemala. Where would you like to go and help?

6. If you have a website, ask your webmaster what it would take to add the logo of your charitable organization as a sign of support.

7. If at the end of the month you find you haven't spent any time volunteering, block off some time next month for such an opportunity.

8. Look back on the month and make a list of the charitable things you did instead, like taking an aging parent to the doctor's office, helping your kids with their homework, or not swearing at the guy who cut you off in traffic.

9. Figure out if the charity of your choice offers monthly automatic withdrawal, which would make life easier for both you and your charity.

10. If you give sporadically, as many people do, and also manage your bank account in a software program,

pull up last year's charitable activity and feel proud of yourself. (You are not allowed to beat yourself with this information, however. If you can't look at it positively, do item 2 instead.)

If you define success as "progress," no matter how small that progress is; and if you define success as "I am a giving person," and then provide yourself with evidence that this is true; and if you define success as "I am willing to view myself as a giving person," and then you take the measurements to support that view, you will apply the inverse Zeno effect and turn on the faucet of two-way giving.

WHEN YOUR MEASUREMENT SYSTEM FOR GIVING IS DEFINED FOR YOU

If you are religious, you may already have a personal measurement system for charitable giving, as most religions have something to say on this matter. The Jewish faith, for example, views the act of giving, or *tzedakah* in Hebrew, as a righteous duty, or religious obligation.

Jews believe there are gradations to giving, and the mixture of willingness, generosity, awareness, and ego embedded in an act of giving can make that act more or less righteous. The levels of tzedakah, from least meritorious to most meritorious, are as follows:

- Giving begrudgingly
- Giving less than you should, but giving it cheerfully
- Giving after being asked
- Giving before being asked
- Giving when you do not know the recipient's identity, but the recipient knows your identity
- Giving when you know the recipient's identity, but the recipient does not know your identity

- Giving when neither party knows the other's identity
- Enabling the recipient to become self-reliant

If you have been raised with a measurement system like this one, you may have a strong desire to continue to honor the traditions of your faith, and that's great. If so, you can apply the inverse Zeno effect as always by using a measurement system like tzedakah to *guide* your acts of giving versus *judging* them.

AMPLIFYING OUR WORLD'S POSSIBILITIES INTO REALITY

I recently visited Alison Austin, the executive director of the Belafonte Tacolcy Center, which provides after-school care in one of the poorest parts of Miami, Florida. While I was there, the center's chief operating officer, Stephanie Sylvestre, told me a story that, for me, captured the essence of what happens when possibility is sucked out of an environment.

"We had an event," she said, "where the kids could buy refreshments. The vendor offered a bottle of water for a dollar, but children who wanted a soda had to take the package deal: the soda, a hot dog, and chips, for two dollars. Most of the kids didn't have two dollars."

Stephanie paused. "Now, if it were you or me, the way we were raised, we would have argued. We would have asked why we couldn't get just a soda for a dollar. We would have at least expressed our discontent — you know, 'Aw, *man!*' Or said something about how unfair it was. But these kids didn't do any of that. They just turned over their dollar and walked away with the water they didn't want. It was the saddest thing I've ever seen."

Alison elaborated. "These kids don't know how to be advocates for themselves. Their parents don't know how to advocate on behalf of their kids, because they've never learned how to be advocates on their own behalf. They're just accepting what's handed to them because they've been conditioned to think they have no options."

Dr. Isaac Prilleltensky, dean of the School of Education at the University of Miami, and author or editor of seven books on community psychology and mental health, backs this up. He says, "We have an ideology — not a science — that you can pull yourself up by your bootstraps. We have these anecdotal stories: I myself am an orphan; I lost my parents at the age of eight. I'm an immigrant. Now I'm the author of many books and have a good job. So why can't you do it?

"Here's why. *The messages that a disadvantaged community receives about itself pathologize its weaknesses rather than reinforce its strengths.* Every member of the community struggles with that pathology. Hoping for individual miracles ends up doing a disservice to the kids. What new stories can we create about succeeding in life?"

Can you see how such messages apply the Zeno effect to the process of change for those communities, rather than the inverse Zeno effect? One of the stories we can create and share is that each of us is a valuable and unique contribution to the planet, no matter where we live, what we have, or who we are. We can believe this about ourselves, and we can help others to believe it about themselves.

We can also embrace our ability to dream, be willing to dream, and treasure and protect the integrity of those dreams, because only through our collective dreams do miracles occur. Spacewalks happen, diseases are cured, war is averted, and people are freed because we dream those things into being. Without our ability to envision a different future, a more desirable future, nothing would change.

Most important, we can accept and cherish our individual capacity as the storytellers of our own lives. Even if we are poor, disabled, or crippled by addiction; even if we are oppressed, mentally ill, or struggling with bad habits, no one can take away our inborn ability to imagine new possibilities for ourselves and our desire to amplify those possibilities into reality. No one, that is, *except ourselves*. We can choose to exercise this power, or we can throw it away. We can apply this science, or we can pretend it doesn't exist. We can allow ourselves to be defined by the world, or we can define our world. When we fall in love with our own ability to choose how to respond to the events in our lives, and we take valuable meaning from them to guide our creative process, we begin to write our own story.

Many times I've been asked, "What if I try really hard, but my dreams still don't come true?" This is always my answer: In the end, do you think you'll be happier if you've lived your life pursuing your dreams or suppressing them?

Dream big. Life is short. Amp it up!

NOTES

CHAPTER 1: CHOOSING WITH THE UNIVERSE

1. Dennis Overbye, "John A. Wheeler, Physicist Who Coined the Term 'Black Hole,' Is Dead at 96," *New York Times*, April 14, 2008, www.nytimes.com/2008/04/14/science/14wheeler.html.
2. William Gibson, "The Science in Science Fiction," *Talk of the Nation*, National Public Radio, November 30, 1999, time code 11:55.

CHAPTER 2: YOUR BRAIN ON CHAOS THEORY

1. You can buy the DVD at the Oil and Water website, www.oilandwaterproject.com.
2. C. Wright Mills, *The Sociological Imagination* (New York: Oxford University Press, 1959), 174.
3. Leonard Bickman, "The Social Power of a Uniform," *Journal of Applied Social Psychology* 4, no. 1 (1974): 47–61.
4. Alyson M. Palmer, "Bizarre 'Strip-Search Hoax' Case before 11th Circuit," Law.com, September 25, 2006, www.law.com/jsp/PubArticle.jsp?id=900005463391.

CHAPTER 3: EPIGENETICS

1. Jeanette Borzo, "The God of Small, Hidden Things," *Wired*, November 2005.
2. Ethan Watters, "DNA Is Not Destiny," *Discover*, November 2006.
3. Sharon Begley, "How Thinking Can Change the Brain," *Wall Street Journal*, January 19, 2007, B1.

CHAPTER 4: DECOHERENCE

1. P. Facchi, S. Tasaki, S. Pascazio, H. Nakazato, A. Tokuse, and D. A. Lidar, "Control of Decoherence: Analysis and Comparison of Three Different Strategies," *Physical Review A* 71, no. 2 (2005).

CHAPTER 5: THE INVERSE ZENO EFFECT

1. W. M. Itano, D. J. Heinzen, J. J. Bollinger, and D. J. Wineland, "Quantum Zeno Effect," *Physical Review A* 41, no. 5 (1990): 2295–2300.
2. B. Misra and E. C. G. Sudarshan, "The Zeno's Paradox in Quantum Theory," *Journal of Mathematical Physics* 18, no. 4 (1977): 756–63.
3. M. C. Fischer, B. Gutiérrez-Medina, and M. G. Raizen, "Observation of the Quantum Zeno and Anti-Zeno Effects in an Unstable System," *Physical Review Letters* 87, no. 4 (2001): 0404021–24.
4. Jim Collins, *Good to Great* (New York: HarperCollins, 2001), 120–22.
5. William Atkinson, "Metrics Drive Success for Major Outsourcing Project," *Purchasing*, January 2004.
6. Joyce Ehrlinger, Self and Social Judgment Lab of Florida State University, www.psy.fsu.edu/~ehrlinger/Self_&_Social _Judgment/.
7. Piers Steel, "We're Sorry This Is Late . . . We Really Meant to Post It Sooner: Research into Procrastination Shows Surprising Findings," *ScienceDaily*, January 10, 2007, www.sciencedaily.com/releases/2007/01/070110090851.htm.
8. Ibid.

CHAPTER 6: AMP UP YOUR WEALTH

1. Quoted in David Ogilvy, *Ogilvy on Advertising* (New York: Vintage, 1985), 15.

CHAPTER 8: AMP UP YOUR LOVE LIFE
AND RELATIONSHIPS

1. Jennifer G. La Guardia and Heather Patrick, "Self-Determination Theory as a Fundamental Theory of Close Relationships," *Canadian Psychology* 49, no. 3 (2008): 201–9.
2. Kristin D. Neff, Kalina M. Brabeck, and Lisa K. Kearney, "Relationship Styles of Self-Focused Autonomy, Other-Focused Connection, and Mutuality among Mexican, American, and European American College Students," *Journal of Social Psychology* 146, no. 5 (October 2006): 568–90.

CHAPTER 10: AMP UP YOUR GIVING
AND COMMUNITY CONNECTION

1. Corporation for National and Community Service, Office of Research and Policy Development, *The Health Benefits of Volunteering: A Review of Recent Research* (Washington, DC: Corporation for National and Community Service, Office of Research and Policy Development, 2007).
2. W. M. Brown, N. S. Consedine, and C. Magai, "Altruism Relates to Health in an Ethnically Diverse Sample of Older Adults," *Journal of Gerontology, Series B: Psychological Sciences and Social Sciences* 60B, no. 3 (2005): 143–52.
3. M. Van Willigen, "Differential Benefits of Volunteering across the Life Course." *Journal of Gerontology Series B: Psychological Sciences and Social Sciences* 55B, no. 5 (2000): S308–18.
4. P. A. Thoits and L. N. Hewitt, "Volunteer Work and Well-Being." *Journal of Health and Social Behavior* 42, no. 2 (2001): 115–31.
5. "Women Empowered: Abay," Phil Borges website, www.philborges.com.

INDEX

ABOUT THE AUTHOR

KIM MARCILLE ROMANER is an expert on the science of amplifying possibility into reality, and on the practical applications for both people and businesses.

If you're looking for Kim, you may find her expanding her comfort zone by driving a stock car, jumping off the tallest building in New Zealand, or rappelling three hundred feet into a cave system. She's also worked in the newspaper industry, which is almost as risky. During her twenty-five years in possibility leadership, her work has ranged from small business ownership to Fortune 500 executive experience. Founder of Possibilities Amplified, Inc., Kim is a popular motivational speaker and sought-after consultant. She has delivered programs for a large variety of audiences and organizations, igniting them with her message of possibility and empowerment.

Known for her ability to teach others to see undiscovered possibilities, craft strategies to take measurable advantage of them, and inspire with a compelling vision, Kim is passionate about

helping people, businesses, and communities transform themselves. She's also starting a day camp for the possibility impaired.
To find out more about Kim's keynote presentations and seminar
programs, and to receive her free Possibility Tips newsletter, you
can contact her at:

Kim@PossibilitiesAmplified.com
Possibilities Amplified, Inc.
415 East Shoreline Drive
North Augusta, SC 29841
Phone: 706-955-0077/305-439-9326
www.possibilitiesamplified.com